Autism and Sensing

22. MAY 02 DEC

D1615139

30131 03539746 9

LONDON BOROUGH OF BARNET

of related interest

Asperger's Syndrome
A Guide for Parents and Professionals
Tony Attwood
ISBN 1 85302 577 1

Reweaving the Autistic Tapestry
Autism, Asperger's Syndrome and ADHD
Lisa Blakemore-Brown
ISBN 1 85302 748 0

Attention Deficity/Hyperactivity Disorder
A Multidisciplinary Approach
Henryk Holowenko
ISBN 1 85302 741 3

The ADHD Handbook
A Guide for Parents and Professionals
Alison Munden and Jon Arcelus
ISBN 1 85302 756 1

Through the Eyes of Aliens
A Book about Autistic People
Jasmine Lee O'Neill
ISBN 1 85302 710 3

Discovering My Autism
Apologia Pro Vita Sua (with Apologies to Cardinal Newman)
Edgar Schneider
ISBN 1 85302 724 3

From Thoughts to Obsessions
Obsessive Compulsive Disorder in Children and Adolescents
Per Hove Thomsen
ISBN 1 85302 721 9

Children with Autism, Second Edition
Diagnosis and Interventions to Meet Their Needs
Colwyn Trevarthen, Kenneth Aitken, Despina Papoudi and Jacqueline Robarts
ISBN 1 853 02 555 0

Pretending to be Normal
Living with Asperger's Syndrome
Liane Holliday Willey
ISBN 1 85302 749 9

Autism: An Inside-Out Approach
**An Innovative Look at the Mechanics of 'Autism'
and its Developmental 'Cousins'**
Donna Williams
ISBN 1 85302 555 0

Autism and Sensing
The Unlost Instinct

Donna Williams

Jessica Kingsley Publishers
London and Philadelphia

All rights reserved. No paragraph of this publication may be reproduced, copied or transmitted save with written permission of the Copyright Act 1956 (as amended), or under the terms of any licence permitting limited copying issued by the Copyright Licensing Agency, 33-34 Alfred Place, London WC1E 7DP. Any person who does any unauthorised act in relation to this publication may be liable to prosecution and civil claims for damages.

The right of Donna Williams to be identified as author of this work has been asserted by her in accordance with the Copyright, Designs and Patents Act 1988.

First published in the United Kingdom in 1998 by
Jessica Kingsley Publishers Ltd
116 Pentonville Road,
London N1 9JB, England
and
325 Chestnut Street,
Philadelphia, PA19106, USA

Second impression 1999

Copyright © 1998 Donna Williams

Library of Congress Cataloging in Publication Data

A CIP catalo[...] of Congress

B[...]

BOROUGH OF BARNET
PUBLIC LIBRARIES

Cypher Group	30.6.00
	£15.95
CPG7OSG 6/3	

ISBN 1 85302 612 3

Printed and Bound in Great Britain by
Athenaeum Press, Gateshead, Tyne and Wear

Contents

For My Friend 'Tim',
who didn't need to speak the language,
because he felt it

and in memory of my father and grandmother
who never lost their minds
because they probably never
were fully committed
to having them in the first place.

I showed them a world left behind.
They saw it in half pictures.
I handed them self before ego.
Intangibly, they touched it.
I spoke them a way from long ago.
They heard it with deaf ears in half whispers.
I shared a reality in which all things are equal.
In their inequality they tried to grasp it
without concept.
I showed them the evolutionary step they didn't take.
They were divided
and the unquestionability of 'normality', 'reality',
and 'humaness'
existed no more.

Foreword

Anyone who has read my previous books, the autobiographical sequence, *Nobody Nowhere* (Times/Doubleday), *Somebody Somewhere* (Times/Doubleday) and *Like Color To The Blind* (Times), the manual, *Autism; An Inside-Out Approach* (Jessica Kingsley Publishers), or even the book of poetry and prose, *Not Just Anything* (Future Education), will wonder how this book fits in. Does it fall somewhere between autobiography, autism and art?

Autobiography is the illustration of learning and experience drawn from the most personal and intimate of experiences. A good autobiography doesn't just write what happened, the external reality, nor confuse how one should have or wanted to have felt or thought with how one actually did. A good biography is not once or twice removed, but direct and felt, experienced and, one hopes, comprehended too, to the core of one's being. When conveyed, a good autobiography gets beyond the surface to that place where realities, experiences, are captured by others – self in other and other in self. I hope that, though not an autobiography, this book has some of this.

Autism is a label which describes outer behaviours, not inner realities. It can appear, disappear and reappear in varying degrees in different circumstances. In other words, depending on strategies and adaptations, it can exist even though it is not apparent and, as appearances can also be misleading, it can appear where it is not in fact experienced. The word autism is, therefore, less substantial, less dependable, than a piece of lint, and I've always tried to express this by using the word enclosed within inverted commas; 'autism', rather than Autism. 'Autism' as an experience describes a very complex interplay between identity, personality, environment, experience and the equipment with which to integrate and make sense of that experience. 'Autism' is simply an internal human 'normality' with the volume turned up. We all have experienced moments when we aren't quite aware or when we are too aware to handle the world. Or moments when we aren't quite aware of the company we are in or so overly aware of it that it gets hard to function. We all have had times when we've had hardly any awareness of our bodies, even been out of them, or felt so in, weighed down by them, that we become hypercritical, eager to escape, tune out, disappear. We have all had times when we've lost the plot, the why, the what or been distracted by the meta-reality inside our heads to the extent that we are suddenly jolted out of a daydream. So too, have we all had moments when we have been so aware that we have taken things in in almost overwhelming, extreme detail. For me, the experience of 'autism' is not of any of these things in themselves, but rather the frequency and extremity with which they are experienced and the degree to which these experiences affect how one expresses oneself and relates to one's inner world and the outer world. It's a matter of whether you visit these states or whether you've lived there. In this sense, this book is not about 'autism' but is enlightened by it.

Art is the ability to convey and, one hopes, affect others in that ability to convey. Art is the ability to capture a feeling, an experience, in a way that is more concise than words alone. It takes you inside the experience rather than speaking to you from outside it. It is an indirect language that addresses the senses as well as the mind. Art finds ways through doors blocked by mind. Any good book should have enough soul to contain some elements of art.

Introduction

It can happen that two people meet and each has a feeling they know each other even though no getting to know has yet happened. You can walk into a house and strongly sense the 'feel' of that house regardless of how its decor attempts to create another, quite different, feeling or impression. You can listen to or watch someone and, regardless of their saying all the right words, making all the right moves, you may sense something that isn't on the surface and somehow doesn't 'fit'. It can happen that you really believe that you ought to be in a certain place at a certain time but find yourself caught up in all sorts of other directions which ultimately prove to have been the 'right' ones in spite of logic to the contrary, as though some inner knowing had directed you; yet this gets called 'coincidence' or 'fate'. It can happen that we find ourselves 'breaking down' with the loss of our façade, left rawly unequipped and exposed at a stage of earlier development which we thought was left behind or well suppressed and consider ourselves 'ill' when we may just have begun, in fact, to get better.

These experiences bring the alternate worlds of 'appear' and 'be' face to face with one another and sometimes into collision. When this happens, most people do what they are trained to do; ignore any sense of the 'be' and rely on what 'appears', in other words upon the learned system of interpretations. For those who can't ignore what they sense, beyond appearances, this can be scary, exciting, confusing, alienating and yet somehow familiar even in the seeming 'foreignness' of these experiences, as though these unusual or rare experiences once came naturally, long before such a time can even be remembered.

This feeling of recognition, of familiarity, that can happen in the first few seconds, without even 'getting to know', can have a feeling of 'coming home' and, so, perhaps, it is just that. Perhaps it comes from a time long ago at the dawn of one's life when the senses are awake to the world for the first time.

Perhaps this feeling comes from a time before the mind, and the egotism which evolves from it, has taken its contorting, sometimes strangulating hold on a free, undistorted, inner self that we are each born with. Perhaps, because this feeling comes from a time before mind, it can be stifled and denied but it cannot be reasoned with on an intellectual level and even if it gives up on what we come to call 'I', ultimately, sooner or later, it breaks through, even if it is suppressed to the last moment of life. It is not as the 'appear' that we leave our bodies, it is as what we were when we entered them. It is as the 'be'.

Perhaps this feeling comes from a time before words, before thought, before interpretation, before competition, before reliance on the conscious mind and before identity, in a time when all new experiences are equal in their worth and there is, as yet, no discrimination and no established sense of boundaries or hierarchy. This is a time when, without boundaries or restriction, one *is* 'the whole world' and everything experienced of that world *is* an indistinguishable and resonant part of one's self with no need to explore it as a separate entity.

If there has ever been a sense of home, a sense of belonging, a sense of equality and harmony, it must be here, for the 'be' is the home we come into the world with and the 'appear' is about the home we learn to construct in its absence. And yet, for most people, the 'be' probably begins to be discarded from the time they are born; perhaps, for some, even sooner. In almost all people, it is gone by the time one seeks to control and limit sensation, when one begins to think, to formulate expression through words, to discriminate and form hierarchies of relative significance and personal significance; as one moves from the system of sensing into the system of interpretation.

Perhaps these first experiences begin to fritter away like leaves scattered to the wind once interpretation begins and meaning starts to evolve a sense of importance. Then, interpretation becomes the road to what most people call 'normality'; a learned and socially constructed road that humans assume sets them apart from animals. And yet, ironically, the lives of many people are then spent sensing, in greater or lesser proportions, that something is missing. Then, they either consciously or unconsciously strive to stifle that 'missing' (the conservative), divert attention from it (the ignorant), or search for that something for themselves and in themselves; that sense of belonging and oneness with the world, that sense of purity and equality and freedom, that stranger who somehow is already 'known' without consciously 'getting to know'. Perhaps, even more than this, here lie questions of God, of self, and the nature and meaning of what people call the 'reality' that is 'life'.

CHAPTER 1

Origins

You probably take it for granted that when you experience yourself, you can at the same time also experience the room you are in, the object you are holding or the person you are with. Most people live in a world in which they can simultaneously experience 'self' and 'other'. Yet at times people lose track of where they are or who they are with or that they are even in company.

At that moment when you look up, embarrassed, to realise you'd started picking your nose without the awareness you weren't alone, you'd slipped out of gear, slipped into the mode of *all self, no other.*

Everyone has had the experience of being so caught up in awareness of another person, a captivating object, an overwhelming surrounding, that you can't remember what you thought or felt or why you were there. You'd slipped into the mode of *all other, no self.* There are moments when you realise you were lost in a limbo, unaware of yourself or anything beyond yourself. This is the state of *no self, no other.*

These are places you have probably visited even though you probably don't remember a time when you lived there. Yet we've all lived there and some of us don't move on and some of us move on but retain a sort of 'foot in both worlds'.

There are some people who live in these foreign realms of all self, no other; all other, no self; or no self, no other or who are constantly jumping between one or the other of these states but never reaching the simultaneous sense of self and other. Those who can't escape one or the other of these realms are sometimes thought crazy, backward, disturbed, loners, obnoxious bores or, if a little luckier, 'creative types'. If they can't escape these realms but have got a tourist visa, able to travel from one mode to another, they are considered anything from frightening to enlightened, from special to weird. We are all some of these things some of the time. Only in degree is it different for these people. They are there either most of the time or all of the time, moving in a social world which, predominantly, is not there. Those who live in these other realms, with or without visitor's visas to the perceptual world most people share, are generally the people who have retained or mastered the system of sensing.

The System of Sensing

When you view someone else, you do not generally view them purely as a collection of sensations, of sensory impressions. Most people bring mind to their experiences of each other. They interpret what they experience.

Unless drunk or on drugs, most people interpret beyond the sensory. They do not perceive themselves as just in the company of fleshy pliable textured material with fibrous stringy matter and moist moving spherical blobs occurring in various colours. Most people gloss over the sensory, unable to see directly the art of life itself and perceive the literal, seeing flesh, hair, eyes, cohesively and collectively forming what they know as human beings.

Most people perceive beyond the literal to the significant. They see they are not just in the company of other humans but in the company of humans they know to be strangers in relations to themselves or in the company of someone they've spent time with or who is related to them or what they call a friend.

Most people perceive objects beyond their grainy, sheeny, reflective, flowing, coloured or opaque appearances, beyond their smooth, raspy, cold, textured tactile experience, beyond the sounds of their chinking, thud-thud, tap-tap surfaces when impacted upon, their sweet, or savoury or chemical tastes or smells, their flexibility, solidness or bounce when bitten into or impacted upon. Most people experience the object before the art of it. They whisk over the sensory into the literal and experience themselves not just in the company of glass, wood, metal, paper, plastic derived objects but beyond this to the significant; that these objects are for cooking, decoration, belong to their neighbour, require a good clean etc.

Most people see past the sensory of the animals and critters they come into company with. They perceive past the staccato movement of numerous fast moving fibrous dark sticks and see spider's legs. Even beyond that they see the spider heading to...for... They see beyond the curved and sheeny tappable surface of black on red with fast moving tiny black sticks beneath, to perceive a ladybird and perhaps consider it a lucky omen. They see beyond the uniformity of silky fibrous lengths from which emanate the sound of 'broook', when made certain contact with and perceive, instead, a cat which responds to stroking, perhaps even that it is their cat or that it hasn't been fed or shouldn't be in the house right now or is walking all over their manuscript.

There are three parts to making sense of experiences of what is perceived as 'other': the sensory, the literal and the significant.

From the 'What' to the 'Why'

The Sensory

In my early to mid childhood, I would hold what was otherwise a comb but perceive a flat, solid form that could be scraped with teeth and into which a very fine indentation could sometimes be made. I would perceive it not by its functional purpose but by its sensory one. It was a 'rih-rih' sounding instrument that would make this sound when run across my teeth. I was living, at least a good part of the time, in the sensory.

What were known as safety pins were solid, difficult to impact upon springy, short lengths of a substance that could bend and would make a tingly sensation when chewed or a delicate, teasing, tinkle noise when quantities of them were shaken (preferably strung together and easy to manipulate as a collective whole) next to the ear.

What were known as patent leather shoes were black smooth, soft pliable reflective and lickable surfaces which would give way under the impact of teeth fairly easily to leave indentations.

A chandelier would become a collective of interacting, seemingly playful sparks of colour, the image of which would trigger the associated sense of the chink-chink sound that would be made if the smooth hard (glass) pieces from which the colours emanated were touched together.

Recently, having moved out of this sensory I looked up at a huge overhead chandelier and remembered the drug-like addictive effect such an experience once had on me. When asked about it, I recalled experiences like it as 'merging with God' because I would resonate with the sensory nature of the object with such an absolute purity and loss of self that it was like an overwhelming passion into which you merge and become part of the beauty itself. It was the ultimate in belonging and 'company'. The feeling was completely compelling and addictive and by comparison the call of the world of interpretation seemed pale, weak, insignificant, foreign and of little reward.

The Literal...

In middle to late childhood I moved beyond seeing the contours and sound and texture of the impact of each grain of grit distinct from the next as it fell through my hand and now saw the literal of 'sand'. I was starting to live in the literal. Yet, when someone told me it was all made by a huge machine and had me put some in my mouth to prove it, I saw nothing odd about doing so nor did I consider its other possible origins. This was the literal but missing the significant. There was no 'I wonder'. I had brought thought to the experience and had the concept 'sand' but I had not brought mind.

Even in my late twenties, still living in the literal, I remember being shown a cardboard cylinder which was the inside of a roll of tin foil. My attention was drawn to the rings around the cardboard cylinder and I was told this was how you could tell how old the cardboard tube was. I'd already heard of this about telling the age of trees and cardboard was from trees so it seemed perfectly logical that this was so. The cardboard cylinder had about five rings going around it so it was, therefore, five years old.

At the age of fifteen, my first job was to put buttonholes into fur coats and as I watched the boss do it, I saw fur being turned and holes inserted. The boss left me to do my job as shown and I did the same, turning the fur and inserting holes. When he returned, he found buttonholes everywhere; in the back panel, in the collar, in the sleeves. I'd got the literal but the significant of the function of the holes or the fashion factor of the exercise had not occurred to me.

Even just two years ago, at the age of thirty-one, I pulled into a parking space which read, 'return prohibited within two hours'. I parked the car and mused over whether I could busy myself for two hours in order not to return. Having finally run out of things with which to fill in my required two hours, I returned nervously to my vehicle, concerned that if I got back into it I'd get fined as I had not yet stayed away for two hours. I decided to do the sensible thing and ask the traffic officer what would happen if I got back into my vehicle. The traffic officer seemed to think I was making a joke when I asked him if he had timed how long I'd been away from the vehicle. I explained the sign and my concern that I had returned to my vehicle within two hours and was afraid I'd now be in trouble. He pointed out that the sign meant I couldn't park, drive away and then park there again within the two hours of the first time I'd parked there.

...and the Significant

At the age of thirty-two, I finally did manage to move from the literal into the significant and it was quite a shock. One of the most striking of these instances was a simple one where I put my cup with the other cups on what I knew, theoretically, was a tea trolley. As I put the cup down, the trolley shelf moved a bit and I put my hand underneath it to push it up and hear the woody noise I expected it would make when I did this repeatedly. As I did this I had the realisation that the shelf was able to move because it was *re*-moveable and that it was re-moveable so it could be cleaned. I jumped back like I'd been greeted by an alien and I felt nervous and a bit scared to find my mind had thought this way. I turned to the person with me and expressed that I was afraid I would lose all the beauty now. For me, the ability to move so quickly from the literal to the significant meant that eventually, I, like most people, would have to struggle to see the sensory which is the art in life itself.

The ability to perceive so naturally the significant in this way also, naturally, becomes a huge part of identity. If the way I perceive changes, then I, too, must adapt in how I identify myself as well as the world around me.

CHAPTER 2

Who's Me?

Ultimately, we are more than how our senses work, more than what our brains do with what's coming in via our senses. Still, it is so easy to confuse 'self' with 'the mechanics of perception or cognition'; our systems.

Ultimately, the self existed before its separability from everything external to it; all entities progressively considered 'other'. Self existed before its various phases of relationship to body or mind and its eventual identification of these. Self existed before the formation of expressed personality or the impact of environment.

Self is essentially none and all of these things simultaneously and yet is, ultimately, a greater force than all of the things with which self is identified; systems, personality, environment, body.

Asked, who am I, my reply is, 'I am a self in the becoming'.

All of us began in the sensory. From here we progressively move towards deeper levels of processing. As we become better able to filter out information not specific to us we become able to focus and choose instead of being drawn indiscriminately and without choice into purely sensory experiences with an absence of 'mind'.

Here, we begin to experience not just life but a sense of our *own* life. We begin to bring concepts to what we see and those concepts become the filters which help us see 'the crowd' instead of this person or this hand or that mouth moving, that help us to see 'the work of art' instead of the pattern on the frame and the lines of the frame and the texture of the canvas and the colour here and there; each fragment held pure, unmuddied from the wider context of the component parts of the whole.

Sometimes, overwhelmed by the weight of mind and existence, some voluntarily take a journey, intentionally or not, back to where they came from, some indulging in drugs or alcohol to take them there. For some, biochemistry mess ups and even the effects of ageing can take them back there without choice.

Losing One's Mind

I was given a doll's house when I was seven. I loved 'it' – the bright red smooth glossy contoured triangular form with the great rih-rih noise made by running the back of the hand over the plastic hollow form which was 'the roof' and the smooth woody tock-tock, slot together hard square white surfaces which were the walls and the collection of plastic chewable forms of various colours, contours and pliability which were the dolls and furniture. I spent my time disassembling the component parts to create the perfection of unmuddied water. The roof, walls, furniture and dolls were kept separate. Later, I used the walls to keep various categories of furniture separate and the dolls all stayed in one category separate from the furniture. Only once I'd unmuddied all the forms could I explore the various structured ways in which the forms could justifiably become muddied according to purpose.

Recently, I saw a young boy who had a bike but would play only with the bright green rubber hand grips or the silver spokes or the black rubber tyres or the shiny black metal frame or the green seat. I was asked why he didn't play with it as 'a bike'. I explained about how, without bringing to the experience the concept of 'bike', it was, perceptually, not 'whole'. My suggestion was that to give it some flow, some cohesion, it could be spray painted matt black so the spokes led to the tyres which led to the frame and the seat and the hand grips to form a sense of the whole from which may come the idea of 'bike'.

Similarly, recently in Italy, after speaking at a conference for the Lion's club, I was given a wall hanging. It had a gold fringe along the bottom of it and brocade running around the side boundaries. Through the top was a metal rod with detachable ends which ran through a satin piece of multi-coloured fabric upon which was some writing and some kind of picture. I took the wall hanging gratefully and disassembled it very quickly, removing the brocade and the fringe, unscrewing the detachable ends from the metal rod running through the top and taking the rod out of the hemline of the fabric. Having separated all the categories, having unmuddied all the waters, I had now turned this collection into something pure and attractive, useful and non-distracting. It was only then that I could clearly see the use of the metal rod and its detachable ends, the use of the fringe and brocade as 'decoration' and, to my surprise, the writing and the picture on the satin now made sense in relation to each other. The writing referred to the picture, describing the place in the mountains portrayed in the satin drawing. It had looked as if I'd destroyed the gift. Only in its disassembly was I able to fully perceive what I'd been given.

Sometimes, these experiences can create a sense of art and also serve to calm or restructure the perception of things. Recently, at a conference of 1500 people, I stood on the stage before them, perceiving every moving part as the audience spoke and moved as they settled into their seats. I was becoming overwhelmed, not holding the movements of one 'human being' in the mental connection of the next. Where someone else may have seen 'crowd', I saw, arm, person, mouth, face, hand, seat, person, eye... I was seeing ten thousand pictures to someone else's one. Then, suddenly, I saw it as multicoloured fluttering rustling leaves that formed the thick bright foliage of a 'people tree' where I, standing in the dark of the stage, was the trunk leading upward and outward to the foliage. Suddenly, the picture had cohesion, even beauty and I began to speak up to the foliage which was the 'people tree'.

Mind's Own Business

People begin to bring mind to their experiences and no longer have to struggle to hear 'words' from spoken sounds. As soon as they hear spoken sounds they bring to the experience the mind concept of, 'oh yes, some words'. Mind itself, the move from preconsciousness into consciousness, provides the greatest tool with which to filter the flood of 'non-relevant' information that would otherwise make simultaneous genius and fool of us all.

Slipping Out of Gear

Under various degrees of stress or overload people can slip out of gear – from the significant back to the literal or further back to the sensory. When we slip back we may find ourselves helpless in a system we left behind before we'd mastered it as a useable and cohesive system. A handful of people can let go the realm of the significant and revisit the literal and such is the mind of many comics.

Disability?

Many people with developmental disabilities live in the sensory, struggling for the literal and among them are some, often unrecognised, great artists and poets. Others, affected less extremely live in the literal, struggling for the significant and among these people are some with quite pure mathematical thinking, inventors and, sometimes, involuntary comedians. I remember in college being asked to work out the percentage of something and asking quite seriously, 'but where's the "of" button'. I remember entering a room to see people looking at a bottle of oil in which was a sprig of some herb. Having asked, 'what is it?', I was told it was a fish tank, so looked hard into the bottle and asked, 'where's the fish?'

In fact, it is sometimes this very nature or a play upon it which either comes naturally or is emulated by so many successful comedians, including people like Rowan Atkinson as Mr Bean, the character in *Some Mothers Do 'Ave 'Em*, John Cleese and Robin Williams.

A handful can let go the realm of the significant or the literal and revisit the sensory; for some this happens under overload where the passing traffic becomes a whirr, the surrounding conversation a jumble. For others, this overload may be brought on by the effects of alcohol of drugs or the involuntary drug-like effects of viral, bacterial or fungal infections; fluctuating blood oxygen or glucose levels; vitamin, mineral or hormonal imbalances; or the effects of food or chemical allergies. When I was about ten years old I used to have a certain colour billiard ball – a pink one. I used to spend around an hour with it before I could reach the point of resonance with it where I would merge with the colour. To anyone else this would have looked like someone 'psychotic' but if they'd known the physical alteration felt in that moment of becoming one with a colour some people would perhaps see it as far less crazy than other ways many people may have spent an hour of their lives at the same age.

I've stood in the street and suddenly had the entire meaning of everything fall away, plunged head first back into the sensory, like falling into an Impressionist painting, the sound around me becoming a chaotic symphony, and in this state, I've felt instant 'called' to the first thing familiar or sensorily addictive. Pink street lights used to do this and in this state I've then been so totally captured and enraptured by the effect of merging with certain pink street lights that it would not have mattered if an oncoming car was headed for me at those moments; I had an express ticket to heaven and I didn't care. I've stood in the railway station and lost track of its purpose, suddenly captured by the sense of symmetry, category and line. I've stood on the highest level of the Eiffel Tower in Paris, lined up in perfection with the symmetry of the city lights stretching out in lines into the forever. I've heard the symphony played by the sound of rain and wind.

This may have been the reality of some great abstract and Impressionist artists, dancers and musicians for whom these things came naturally, without mental application of technique. Others, without being either comics or artists may return to a place for a visit or extended holiday, voluntarily or involuntarily, and find it like a 'homecoming' – a place of already established identity and self.

Body Who?

Think of 'self', and you might think of the mind and consider that what is important is to expand stored knowledge, the accumulation of information, the ability to use mental strategy.

You may think of the body, how a person looks, and consider that if you look 'good' by some transient fashionable culture-bound, time-bound, standard of the time that you are good.

You might also think of the self as the place of feelings expressed through the body in some conventional way or interpreted by mind leading to these feelings being acted upon in life and so self becomes the broken heart of today, the elation of tomorrow.

You might think about self as life lived, the accumulation of experiences, physical journeys, mental torments, emotional struggles.

The self is also about identifying and identifying can be about interpretation. But, before the time of interpretation, identifying and knowing was not about the interpretation of mind. It was about the resonance of 'will'.

CHAPTER 3

The Essence of 'Social'

Before mind was even a notion, before hierarchy and the discrimination born of it, there was will; the realm of selfless-self. In the time before mind, there was no simultaneous sense of self and other. Nor was there a sense of competition. Nor was there the social people-world experience of 'with'. In the time before mind, there is a time even before the experience of 'in front of' and, later, 'at', even before the experience of all self, no other; all other, no self where entity-separateness is established and loneliness is born. Before all this was another time. A place of magic lost.

No Self, No Other

When you experience something external to you, there is the experience of your own boundary. When you experience something, you experience its 'themness'. You experience its boundaries, its separability and separateness from you. Its existence within those boundaries is not just about its appearance, its surface, its physical substance. It is about its 'beingness'; its energy within those boundaries, beyond that appearance, that surface, the external experience of that physical substance. It is possible to experience an entity outside of oneself without taking account of its appearance, its surface or its physical substance. It is possible to be experienced by another entity without it taking account of or experiencing your own appearance, surface or physical substance. The energy bound up in these physical forms can be experienced beyond them, not just when this energy gives up its form, as in death, but in life, too. This energy can escape these boundaries and experience other energies beyond their boundaries just as some can leave their own boundaries and experience yours.

Shadow Senses

Before we learned to use our physical-body senses with intention, we were still able to see, hear, feel with 'shadow senses'. Some people blind from birth, for example, can get about without some of the aids used by those who came to rely on their physical eyes. Some amputees can still feel the pain or itch in a limb that has been cut off. The 'body' is more than a physical form. It is an energy form, generally, but not necessarily, contained and expressed through a physical form.

The first stop on the journey of life is one where nothing has impassable energy boundaries. In a nutshell, the physical can be bypassed by the shadow senses of the non-physical body.

You might ask, how, if being perceived without intentional directed use of the physical body, is there any awareness of such an experience. Where is mind?

In speaking of sensing, 'knowing' is not part of mind's interpretation or ego's imposition of schema. Here, knowing is pure, mathematical, a place of patterns and of system, a place of resonance and its product of mergence.

One does not need words to shadow-sense the coming of pattern changes before hearing the impending changes voiced through a hole in the face or visually cued. Here one does not need to touch an object to feel its nature; the feeling of that nature is not, at this stage, from a place of body separateness, it is to feel the object *as* the object, from within, without interpretation or mind, using the body not as a tool of sensory exploration or body as self, but as a tool of resonance. One does not need to check, judge, analyse, prioritise. The experience simply happens, not because the mind wants it or thinks about it, but because, quite irrelevant of the dictates of mind, it is willed.

Growing Up?

Most people have let go of this phase of development in the first weeks or months of life, leaving progressively redundant their capacity for the knowing and belonging of resonance and merging. They begin to respond with an identity separate from that with which they are drawn into contact. They begin to develop mind and thinking, to bring concept to their experiences and through this to filter information.

For some people, this transition is slower, so that identification with this early phase is stronger. For some, too 'awake' in this phase, the mastering of this as a system could bring such established security in it to easily let it go with the welcoming in of a new developmental phase.

Some, perceiving themselves as under extreme continual threat or fearful of foreignness or lacking curiosity for the new, may cling to the first state they knew as home. Some may not feel ready for the weighty plod-plod of body connectedness. Others, deeply sensual and 'artistic', may feel it too unnatural to let go of this ultimate capacity to capture the experience – *as* it.

Although I gradually tasted later phases, I was still fully functioning in this earlier phase when I was in late childhood. Until I was about seven or eight, I was still privately sure I could walk through walls or solid surfaces, perhaps because I had the experience from an earlier time.

Recently, I was speaking to a man who'd had similar constant out-of-body experiences in childhood who spoke about the confusion of whether he'd left with a body or without and the occasional grip of panic at finding himself outside the physical body and afraid he may not be able to get back in.

I had a memory from the age of about three where I'd got up into the hall cupboard and stepped out but not landed. I'd found myself about a foot off the floor and I was afraid I couldn't get back down. I had willed myself back down to about two inches off the floor before finally landing. I had then gone back to bed. I'd remembered this not as a dream but as a memory, feeling vividly the body-memory of the feeling of the wood of the cupboard in my hand and the sense of space around me. Perhaps, without having good ongoing connection to my physical body, I was having an out-of-body experience at the time and was using shadow senses which I had confused with physical-based senses.

I also remember responding to people's call by coming into the room, sometimes answering their request by going and getting what they'd wanted. People had seemed surprised at these behaviours because they hadn't spoken the requests. It didn't occur to me that I hadn't been verbally called or asked or that I was busy with things of my own at the time. At these times, I suppose, I was 'out of my mind'.

As I got older, I took this surprise or disturbance at this 'ability' to mean that I'd broken the convention and I had to wait until these things had come from people's mouths instead.

When responding at these times, I was in a kind of dream state and it is possible that in this state one can sense the intention of will before it is channelled through mind into the expression via body; basically a phone line which gets through more quickly. Preconsciousness is like a post-hypnotic state where information cannot be accessed but can be triggered and verbal or visual language which requires interpretation addresses the accessing of the conscious mind, not the triggering mechanism of the pre-conscious state.

One of the other assumptions that happens in this state is that there is no need to articulate or indicate because it is assumed that others, too, can use these mechanisms. But, like lazy, wasted, unworked muscles, others may still have these mechanisms but the well developed, well worked mechanisms of conscious accessing and interpretation step in to take over.

The system of no self, no other is one which does not require the use of body. It has its uses. Living through one's body, one loses the ability to feel what it is to *be as* that cake even though one can now use body to pick up the cake and eat it. 'Socially', the system of no self, no other is one not of 'with', nor 'at' nor 'in front of' but of 'as'. This state, though mindless, is the place where the soul is in its purest state before the contortions of mind; a place of total objective subjectivity, before hierarchy or prejudgement.

All Self, No Other; All Other, No Self

We move from the pure, essentially egalitarian, boundaryless realm of no self, no other where we have belonging among all things. As we do, so, too, do we move away from the 'God' in all things as we move into the life that most human beings have evolved and formalised and passed on to new travellers. From no self, no other to a fluctuating state of all self, no other; all other, no self, egotism is born and resonance becomes progressively more discriminate and redundant in a system which promotes its redundancy.

This second state begins for most people in the first weeks or months of life and most begin to leave it for the next phase – that of simultaneous self and other – between around two and five years old.

Like the earlier, boundaryless, phase of no self, no other, some are late moving out, identifying self too strongly with the systems of all self, no other; all other, no self, mastering its mechanics, its strategies and adaptations for navigation in a world based on simultaneous self–other.

Some, hooked on autonomy and privacy, fearful of social-emotional affect, avoidant of connection, may prefer this stage of 'in front of' and 'at', having an aversion to the interpersonal stage of 'with' which comes with simultaneous self–other.

Some, purist in their insistence on not allowing the waters to muddy, geared for order and category, for control and system, may find all self, no other; all other, no self, more comprehensible, more natural, more tidy, than the muddied water of simultaneous self–other.

In the state of all self, no other, I could perceive myself as a person and it was totally natural to express this self equally aimed at a tree as at an animal, object, person, the wind or nothing at all.

In the state of all self, no other, all action is perceived as being from self, to self. It is not a social state of 'with', nor even 'at'. It is a state of 'among' and 'in front of'.

In this state, when expression was aimed at other, the sense of other remained theoretical, an impression, not held within the same simultaneous context as self. So selfhood remained whole but the sense of other was partial.

The sense of other can cause a switch to the opposite state, able now to perceive a whole sense of other but robbed of a simultaneous sense of self; it is as though the approach of other causes the self to disappear. Information continues to be accumulated but as though accumulated not by self but by a computer now devoid of self. The 'thank you', the 'please', the perception of having been given something or being meant spontaneously to act upon hints are like colour to the blind in this state. In this state, you exist in relation to you even if your actions are aimed at me, just as my actions, even aimed at you, are felt to be from me to me, only allowing you to observe or hear. Call this the state of the egotist or the sociopath, it is a pure state in which the psychological game playing, comparison and competition of simultaneous self and other has not yet started up.

For some, insistent on staying in this phase and hooked on existence, it may become important to stay only in all self, no other, avoiding the switch that would cause the loss of experience of self. For others, hooked on non-existence, swimming in the purity of affectless information accumulation, the state of all other, no self, life as a walking information accumulation centre is preferable.

It is in the switch from sensing to interpretation that the system of all self, no other; all other, no self, begins and it is here also that body as a tool of sensory exploration begins to be put firmly in place. Here, the foundations of relating socially through bodies begins and being in the company of objects and creatures becomes progressively demoted down the rungs of hierarchy in a world governed by formalised and systematised human values. These values simultaneously call us forward and burn the bridges behind us.

Here we have little body consciousness for body is a tool and we begin to seek company with other humans on a sensory based level, clutching at the straws of interpretation from which mind and mind's meta-self are born.

Simultaneous Self–Other

Some people can look at food and their mouth waters, look at someone and feel sexually aroused or smell something and know how it is going to taste. I could hear a sound and physically sense the tactile nature of the object, look at it and sense the sound that would come from it or exactly how it would catch or refract light.

We move from no self, no other to all self, no other; all other, no self and from there into simultaneous sense of self and other – the place of 'with' in which we discover comparison, reflection and the competition and hierarchy born of it. As we do this we move from body as a tool of resonance into body as a tool of sensory exploration into body as self through which we express ourselves socially. We develop a sense of social and communicative self and of a personal and internal relationship to body, not as separate to it and often no longer even separable from it.

Here we see ourselves not trapped within body but coming through it like a vehicle for the self within and an extension of that self. Then, with fashion and other often illogical social learning, we begin to shape the expression not of who we are, but of who we think we should be or wish we were and so seal our path as we move away from both true self and the life path that would have sprung from that self which some call destiny.

As we develop, expression, which should spring naturally, diminishes as it is sold out and replaced by stored movements, lines, voices, stored thoughts, wants, likes, and even thoughts about thoughts which are often accessed so much more quickly than connected true expression. This can be especially compounded when true connected expression is blocked by anxiety, accessing problems, guilt, shame, denial, fear, an overwhelming sense of one's differentness or the need for acceptance.

Here, as we begin to construct false 'self', we become demi-gods but we lose company with our first and most basic security – our sense of connected real self. We begin to know inferiority and the possessiveness born of it. We begin to know emptiness and attempt to fill time or bury our heads in the sand. We begin to mistake control for caring, possession for self-worth, defensiveness for strength, dependence for love, submission for respect, and compulsion and obsession for like, want and choice. Here we find our politics and religion, our economics and other God-replacements as we become part of society. In death we again let go of body and return to no self, no other in the great belonging of collective mergence of energies no longer confined to the varied physical forms they clung to. 'In my end is my beginning', wrote T.S Eliot.

CHAPTER 4

The Everything of Nothing

Up to the age of four, I sensed according to pattern and shifts in pattern. My ability to interpret what I saw was impaired because I took each fragment in without understanding its meaning in the context of its surroundings. I'd see the nostril but lose the concept of nose, see the nose but lose the face, see the fingernail but lose the finger. My ability to interpret from what I heard was equally impaired. I heard the intonation but lost the meaning of the words, got a few of the words but lost the sentences. I couldn't consistently process the meaning of my own body messages if I was focusing in on something with my eyes or ears. I didn't know myself in relation to other people because when I focused processing information about 'other', I lost 'self', and when I focused on 'self', I lost other. I could either express something in action or make some meaning of some of the information coming in but not both at once. So crossing the room to do something meant I'd probably lose the experience of walking even though my body did it. Speaking, I'd lose the meaning of my own sounds whilst moving. The deaf–blind may have lost their senses; I had my senses but had lost the sense. I was meaning deaf, meaning blind; interpretation and the realm of mind wasn't a reliable or consistent system for me. I remained reliant far longer than most people on an earlier system: the system of sensing.

Even once interpretation got progressively on line (better late and slow than never) I couldn't let go what I trusted and identified with. I can remember walking down the street even at the age of six and sensing something which was about to happen but then attempting to read (interpret) the situation. I remember, at that time, that I turned from sensing and went with the odds of what I'd interpreted and that it hadn't worked out. What I'd sensed had been right. I recall cursing myself for not trusting in sensing and attempting to use interpretation.

Being Trained Out of Sensing

As people grow up, there's a huge pressure not to sense but to use 'common sense', which is to use the system of interpretation. Both interpretation and sensing have equally their advantages and disadvantages. To lose one system is a tragedy to the worth, creativity and feeling of belonging this world might otherwise know; a place where fashion, hierarchy and pre-judgement are not God's creations but those of humans who have allowed these things to govern them. Had the system of sensing not become so globally redundant in adults, religion, the concepts of life and death, of physics and science, of language and of the social would not be the black and white 'realities' they are perceived to be.

Ideally people could use either system flexibly as required, even to test one against the other just one would test taste against smell to back-up the perception of one with the other before trusting to eat. Instead, so many people lose the capacity to sense and then confuse the conscious interpretation of mind with the preconscious sensing of will. Many so-called 'psychics' will constantly seek feedback and adjust what they claim to sense accordingly. Many are so tuned in to the conscious, to analysis and interpretation, that they cannot get out of mind enough to get into will. Anyone who worries or checks continually whether they are on the right track or not in what they claim to 'sense' cannot have mind out of the picture enough to be able to tune in to will with any consistency. Even the expression of what is sensed at the level of will comes out automatically, without accessing, monitoring or alteration and most so-called 'psychics', even if able to tune into will, cannot tune mind out of the preconscious triggered expression of what has been sensed.

In relying on what I call 'the system of sensing', the realm of 'will', which doesn't follow intention, is drawn to that with which it resonates.

In my teens, I lived in quite a dangerous and lonely state a lot of the time and this caused me to 'visit' non-physically people and places where I felt safe. I didn't do this with imagination. I didn't fantasize what I'd like to say or do. I simply found myself feeling physically in these places or with these people. I could not see myself there and I did not interact with the people I'd been drawn to. Yet I did feel myself moving up the stairs to my friend's flat, through the front door and into the kitchen. I could sense the smell of the room and the noises in the room. I could 'hear' and 'see' as my friends moved about and went on with things.

What I'd seen and heard was generally quite trivial; someone doing the dishes, getting something to eat, going to bed. What had surprised me was that, upon checking with these friends without prompting them about what I'd experienced, the events had apparently happened in the same order in which I'd seen them at the time I'd 'been there'.

Two of the strangest experiences among these were one when I 'visited' my friend but found myself in a different house. I moved from room to room and found what felt like her room. When I saw her again she told me she'd moved house and I told her I knew. She was surprised at this and asked how. I described the house and the layout of the rooms and my description had been precisely in accordance with where the family had moved. The other experience was after leaving a house I'd lived in for two years. In the two months before I'd left I'd moved bedrooms and had stayed in one with a sliding door. After having left, I continued to dream that I was living in that house. About a year later I saw the person who remained living there who proclaimed I'd 'never left'. I asked what this meant and was told that for some time afterwards, every morning, around the time I'd usually get up, the door would slide itself open. It occurred to me then that what others called 'ghosts' were possibly sometimes merely unintentional out-of-body experiences. It occurred to me, further, that some of the entities having out-of-body experiences may have had no living bodies to return to but perhaps didn't realise or accept this, thinking perhaps they were merely dreaming and couldn't wake up. Perhaps other such 'visitors' had living physical bodies they were just out of at the time, able to separate from them either in a waking dream state or sometimes in a sleeping one. Some have had these experiences in death before being brought back to life. Some have had these experiences when in a coma or state of temporary unconsciousness. Occasionally, someone more 'usual' just has them, asleep, and sometimes even 'awake'.

This mind versus will, intention versus resonance, interpretation versus sensing, appear versus be, is all strange language to most people. Yet, if what follows seems to the minds of some readers to be alien then it is probably because I am talking about experiences we have all had, and yet most left behind before many can even remember.

'Me'

Back then, back in the beginning in the time before mind, 'I' was not my body nor even considered my selfhood necessarily to exist there. There was me and there was the thing others might have called 'my body' but there was no feeling that this thing belonged to me and the concept that it was actually part of me was a very difficult one to grasp in more than just theory. As far as I experienced, there was a thing stuck on me, encasing me (at times claustrophobically) and I couldn't physically leave it behind no matter how fast I ran away from it, attacked it or sought to shut out awareness of it.

It is, at this point, useful to point out that here the term 'I' is not the 'I' of the mind but the 'I' before the mind, a sort of 'I' that is the will.

My will learned to escape 'body' very young, certainly before the age of three. It remained where I'd left it, zombie-like, and 'I' floated outside of it not too far away. Sometimes, my will was dragged back to it via emotion and empathy at what was happening to it and sometimes because its bodily needs created a sense of pressure to return but mostly, there was body and there was 'me' (in the sense of 'me' as will, not as mind) and we were separable; able to join forces or not.

These are scary things for many people. There is much horror and mythology associated with out-of-body experiences, merging and the idea of a spirit as separate from mind or body. Stories of ghosts, witches, vampires, telepathy, telekinesis and, of course, madness, are enough to make many people avoid thinking about where some of this mythology may have been derived from and sends others, curious and often power seeking, heading toward so-called 'psychics', 'mediums' and cults. Others seeking or fearing what they see as 'powers' and either actually having no capacity for, or refinement of, these systems, have succumbed to mental disturbance or so-called madness as they seek these things with mind and false self. In a world of Clive Barker and Stephen King novels, how can the mechanics of earlier systems be openly discussed in an atmosphere so tainted with superstition and issues of power, status and false self? In discussing these things recently with a man for whom mergence, out-of-body experiences and the system of sensing was still a fully functioning system about which he could talk fluently, I'd felt nervous that others would have heard such a discussion and I warned him to explain how these things worked, not just recall the experience. 'Be careful', I told him, 'Always tell the mechanics. People hear with Stephen King ears.'

The Realms of Resonance

Just as 'will' could join with body or not, 'will' could join with all sorts of other things. 'Will' could sense the wall or the surface, texture and density of material without looking at it with physical eyes or touching it with physical hands or tasting it with a physical tongue or tapping it to hear its sound. It was as though some part of 'me', of my 'be-ing' could see without my eyes, hear without my ears, touch without my hands and feel bodily without my body making direct physical contact. It was as though 'I' had two sets of senses, the physical ones, and non-physical ones which some people have termed 'shadow senses'.

Perhaps these non-physical senses were like a functioning neurological imprint of each of my physical senses, just as the brain has an imprint of each limb. Perhaps, just as some people experienced pain in phantom limbs after amputation, this imprint of the senses could work even in the absence of using my physical ones but only so long as 'I' had not developed reliance on those physical senses. Some people, blind from birth, have retained the use of a shadow-sense. It is this 'shadow-sense' with which they can sometimes sense the boundaries of a room even without reliance purely on sonics, the sudden entry of something new into it without hearing or smelling it or a change in the feel of the room without being told.

I have vague recollections of being able to sense the surfaces around me. I have a sketchy sense of having been able to sense the wall and changes in its structure where some parts were more solid than others. I recall sensing this without looking or using touch, changes such as where a door or window broke up or changed the continuity. I recall a sort of 'resonance' with matter, a kind of non-physical 'body mapping'.

Now that may sound crazy if you've never lived it or grew out of it before this system of sensing ever evolved in any complex way. For a lot of people this will be in the heebie-jeebie pile along with spiritual healing and 'feeling the vibes'. But if I was an alien it would not be judged as crazy even if its foreignness would scare some people and fascinate others. It is certainly true that I've lived an 'alien' life.

I can remember 'losing myself' in the wall when I was around six months old. I know I was around that age because I was still in a cot and I hadn't really started using my body with conscious control.

I say, 'losing myself' because in becoming resonant with something else, you lose connection with your separateness to that thing. Suddenly, there is no you and what had been you just becomes a tool, like a sponge through which this sensing or resonance is taken in.

What is sensed is not taken in by the conscious mind and there is no thought and no reflection, no wonder and no curiosity. There is just a journey into whatever is being sensed and an accumulation of what has been 'mapped out'. What is mapped out is the 'feel' of the experience and it is mapped out as a series of uninterpreted patterns and all variations in that first pattern. It is not thought about and there is no conscious awareness going on. It is like living inside a light bulb; a vacuum. Thought continues but it continues beyond the accessible grasp of the conscious mind, within the triggerable realm of unknown-knowing; the preconscious mind.

The question is, can those who outgrew this ever return to this state once they've achieved an ongoing, consistent and permanent grip on consciousness? Perhaps those who have a tentative hold on it (e.g. some people with sleep disorders, epilepsy or certain developmental disabilities which may interrupt the capacity consistently and cohesively to interpret sensory experience), may be more likely to hold on to this system beyond infancy, even into adulthood in spite of social structures which promote its progressive but speedy redundancy.

Remnants

We are chastised for not 'paying attention', told 'look at me when I'm speaking to you', 'use your common sense', 'think before you act'; all of which are acts of conscious awareness using the system of interpretation. But just what were we, perhaps, otherwise doing when we were not doing these things?

Often, when not 'paying attention', people are daydreaming. Sometimes this is fantasy of the conscious mind and sometimes the person is not aware of daydreaming until called back to consciousness. Where then was the person?

Daydreams can be fantasy, conscious and within immediate accessible grasp and able to be monitored as they happen. Daydreams which are preconscious can usually not be monitored at the time they are happening even though people can catch themselves there as return to the mode of the conscious mind returns.

There are also some people who have occasionally developed a rare adaptation to living in the preconscious state; the ability to use multiple states of consciousness. In other words, to 'listen in on' or 'watch' their own preconscious daydreams or thoughts.

I remember this mechanism switching on and off because it is a tentative balance; it is the hard to maintain centre point on the see-saw where it balances in the middle. If consciousness kicks in too forcefully, it closes out access to the preconscious and the capacity to monitor it or allow its expression out freely through the body. If preconsciousness has too tight an hypnotic grip, if the state is too deep, then consciousness is closed out and there is no knowledge of what is known. The connection of preconscious expression with body and through body is often disconnected in this state because body connectedness itself is a major jolting mechanism which causes self-awareness that causes a shift from the preconscious to the conscious, often losing the connection between the two. For someone like me who found the constant shifts disturbing and alienating to my sense of cohesion and sense of self, I fought for that cohesion as a matter of soul survival. At the same time, living in the preconscious state can cost the ability to function via body and that's what's required for communication, interaction and independence within the social structures of this world as most people know it. To allow consciousness to come in too strongly, when having lived so wholly in the preconscious, then, equally, would have left me stranded; able to function but with nothing driving me would be as bad as having all the drive disconnected from the mechanisms through which this can be expressed in some functional and observable way through the body. Others who made the fast developmental transition from living in the semi-awake state of preconsciousness to living in the waking state of consciousness wouldn't face this dilemma.

Even having achieved the capacity to balance the see-saw in the middle, I became able to do many things but still found it a long road to doing others. I could eventually monitor my own out-of-body experiences, monitor my own mergence with the feel of things around me, and eventually even dream in my sleep with the mechanism of running a simultaneous commentary about the reality or unreality of the dream. I developed the capacity to switch the dream off if it was too bizarre, confusing or disturbing to my own sleeping mind.

Being able to allow preconscious expression out via body and monitor it meant this expression was still not controlled or directed by mind. I could speak and move and take action but developed a clear sense of the dissonance between the expressed actions of preconscious will versus those intended by conscious mind. Mind was often distressed by how will was expressing different or opposite to how mind itself would have got expression out. Mind was also often alienated and distressed to find who was in there when actions and expression had come out without conscious intention, or even awareness of some of this. To my mind, it was like being possessed but simultaneously awake to see it, and in late childhood onwards when that unknown knowing was really coming out in bursts in a big way, I was very very frightened by the deep, rich, poetry which emerged from what I knew as a shallow person without much thought at all. I burned much of it and hid it from myself as much as anyone else. I was ashamed of being discovered as being possessed when the first paintings and drawings which emerged from me were full of symbolism and intricacy, in spite of me being mentally very very concrete. I first hid these, then covered them with black paint so I could no longer see them. My mind, unable to accept these as expression of 'me' had to obliterate them from existence and awareness to relax, unthreatened by any challenge to identity. The first musical compositions which emerged from me around the age of fourteen frightened me in their passion and capacity to move. To my mind, these were not 'me' because I feared feelings and didn't acknowledge them directly as mine. I buried them, in shame, not playing them for anyone till I was twenty-two. My first autobiography (around 250 pages) which came out of me at the age of twenty-six was written in four weeks and became a bestseller but as it came out I felt like a robot, not attempting at all to plan or consciously access anything which was coming out, just eager to get finished with the compulsive and frightening purge of its emergence. For me there was a huge difference between the internal 'I' of will and the external 'I' of mind. The two took a long time to be willing and accepting of meeting each other, creating a lot of difficulties in relating and expressing myself and forcing me into all sorts of contortions and corners, freed in some and totally restricted in others.

I had to reconcile myself to the understanding that as I fluctuated between preconscious expression with conscious intention stifled and conscious expression with preconscious expression stifled and even denied, that 'I' was, in fact, both of these. The only difference between me and most other people was that I was able to become quite fully aware of being both. Most people are either unaware or have a sense of this 'other' within themselves but are so afraid, ashamed or nervous of it or fear the consequences of the loss of control that its release would entail that these two sides never come face to face in battle, nor its resolution.

It took me a long time to trust the expression of the ghost within me, a long time to see past the Stephen King mentality which teaches us to fear such mechanisms and enshroud them in mythology. It took a long time to see that the preconscious state, uncontaminated and uncompromised by the intention of the conscious mind and the contortions of false self is actually a very pure state and that if a monster exists, it is probably that which exists suppressed and controlled within the conscious mind rather than within the preconscious state which is the realm of the soul.

Sometimes, 'daydreams' are not of the imagination, conscious or preconscious. Sometimes, they are out-of-body journeys into other times or places where you might find out later that you 'witnessed' something happening elsewhere or that happens at some later time. Some people are more able to retain awareness or monitoring of this preconscious state. These are the people said to be 'psychic'. Others don't recall these journeys

at the time but experience 'deja vu' regarding places they've never physically been, people they've never physically met or sequences of sensory
experiences they didn't have in their physical body and yet which feel as
though they had been previously experienced.

Some people have more of these 'psychic' experiences or 'deja vu' regarding the people closest to them. This is because energy boundaries are
not as closed to those we are closest to and trust most. We 'have our guard
down' more with them than with others, not just mentally, emotionally or
physically, but 'energetically', spiritually. Some people are not consistently
or cohesively in their bodies so their energy boundaries are more 'open'
than for most people, regardless of trust and closeness. These are the people most prone to a wider range of 'psychic' experiences and 'deja vu', having visions of lives, places, times, unconnected to their own. Different
things affect energy boundaries differently. In the same way as experience
interacts differently with every different personality, every different collection of past learning experiences, so too different experiences interface
differently with different energy boundaries. Like personality, it would be
hard to test or control for in the way one would test with an issue of mind
or cognition. One is a photograph, the other an abstract work of art.

The resonance which causes the ability to perceive, consciously or preconsciously, happenings in other times or places is something which will
interplay with personality and experience. Trust and closeness are more
likely to provoke 'resonance' in people who have some warmth and 'openness'. The purely empathic person may resonate easily with energies
which are like its own, whether strangers or not. Some insecure or power
hungry people are attracted to the powerful or to what they fear and might
be likely to resonate with 'negative' happenings. For a long time, having
seen these qualities in some people, I became afraid of the system of sensing, convinced it was a 'bad' thing because so many such people were
drawn to explore it. Fortunately, purely insecure and power hungry people
are generally more drawn to the use of mind than will and it is this which
closes them out of the ability to master the system of sensing. Since realis-
ing this, I feel it is far more likely that those who would be most likely to
master the system of sensing are those who have some kind of 'purity' of
spirit at some level, something not likely in those dominated by insecurity
and desire for power.

'Look at me when I'm speaking to you', 'use your common sense',
'think before you act', are all common expressions which are part of the
counter-culture to the system of sensing. Those who live in the preconscious are more likely to use their senses peripherally and take in a wider

range of information but to do so without the judgement of mind. Forcing these people to look directly, give directed feedback that they had been listening, or respond verbally and directly in an interactive and immediate way, jolts them from preconsciousness back into the conscious mind. Many people have found they can tune in better with many things going on at once. These people absent themselves from the directness of what they are taking in and can then take it in more peripherally and precon- sciously, taking in a wider context. Others, who use a much more con- scious and narrow focus go the other way, needing to close out background information in order to make conscious meaning out of what they are tuning in to. Some maintain both systems and fluctuate between the two.

So-called 'society' operates on a directly-confrontational approach. It's an 'in your face' world. This directly-confrontational approach is rein- forced with emphasis on manners and conventions which force constant tuning in to consciousness. This forces human beings to live most of their lives relying on ten per cent of their brains at the expense of all they might otherwise express, discover, know, if society used an indirectly- confrontational system which allowed people to use the ninety per cent they generally don't use. The irony of this is that preconsciousness is a state of subjective objectivity. Yet society which pays lip-service to the value of objectivity, forces its members into the constant subjective state of the conscious mind.

The constant insistent one-sided emphasis on 'paying attention', see- ing 'daydreaming' as a waste of time, the emphasis on 'look at me when I'm speaking to you' may be eroding the sacred within us all.

Cognitive Mechanics

When the system of sensing came naturally to me, 'I' was purely will and had little, if no, conscious mind. Because of an allergy-induced state, I ap- peared deaf and oblivious to pain and even when reactiveness could be sparked, the conscious decisiveness of mind could not. This meant I lived in a relatively constant sleepwalking state, a bit like a zombie, learning to function solely on 'auto-pilot' according to the reactive triggering of stored information. Unlike most other children of around the same age, in the absence of much of a conscious mind, this preconscious will-state of functioning was the only one I knew.

Relying on the conscious mind has the benefit of accessing informa-tion with intention. The preconscious state, on the other hand, relies on triggering, like post-hypnotic suggestion.

The conscious mind has the benefit of creating something and experi-encing one's separateness from it during the process with the by-product of self-consciousness and inhibition. The preconscious state involves no such inhibition so what comes out is unrestricted and sometimes 'genius' but may involve the by-product of alienation from the process. As one merges with the process and can only experience the product the process lacks the experience of intention or applied effort and monitoring as *sepa-rate* to it. In this state it is hard to feel one created the product except by de-duction or upon reflection.

I didn't 'learn' with any conscious application how to sculpt, yet as soon as I began, I could sculpt with a lot of skill, producing as my third piece of work after six weeks of sculpting, a detailed life sized nude which later got cast in bronze. I did not paint in the art classes at school, yet when, as an adult, I did finally dare to use colour and brushes, the works I pro-duced were like those of an artist who'd been painting for years. I didn't study how to write and had barely handed in any expressive written work other than purely academic replies to set topics. Yet when I sat down to type out the story of my life, both my first and second instalments became international best-sellers, not after trying for the right publisher, but seem-ingly 'by chance'. As soon as I sat at a piano, without a single music lesson, I could play classical music and immediately composed my first piece of what is now over a hundred pieces of music. The poetry that found its way out of me around the age of ten frightened me in its depth and foreignness. I didn't know myself to have any depth. It is now published and some of it considered very highly within its field. I never sang in music class, yet I can sing in a voice many would be proud of. These skills have been labelled 's-avant skills', said to affect around ten per cent of people with 'autism' while the majority of 'savants' have autism. Yet these labels tell nothing of the mechanics of these skills and the question is not so much why some have got them but why they retained them where others let them go before ever discovering they had them.

My awareness of what was happening when producing these things was a bit like the awareness one might have listening in and watching one's own dreams with the exception that my body was awake and there was no dream happening. Perhaps this is comparable to the experiences of some people who faint or have seizures but maintain a sense of what has happened to their body or the responses of others around them at the time.

Similarly, in near-death experiences, there have been reports of people be-ing able to 'see' or 'hear' or 'feel' in the absence of consciousness or in the absence of any use of physical body senses.

Back in these early days as more or less pure 'will', 'I' had no conscious mind-self and none of the boundaries of 'self' and 'other' which come with that.

Without mind, in the uninterpreted sensory experience of what is called 'the wind' I'd be seen 'off-line' seeming to be staring into space and I felt caught up in the swirl and movement around as though it moved through me and I moved through it till we were a part of each other. I could 'resonate' with this entity or with the flow of water, able to feel my-self running free with it and surprised to return to my body.

I could merge with a colour or shape just as two instruments may reso-nate with one another when in proximity. I would stare at the side edge of an irridescent green ruler at the angle where it caught the light with per-fection and I would eventually become progressively ecstatic as the point of mergence approached and, in an energy sense, I 'became' the colour it-self.

Caught up in the patterns of these entities during this resonance, and without having evolved any inseparable connection to my own entity, 'I' became at times disconnected from any sensing of the patterns of 'my' body; its breathing and heart beat, and even its body sensations or emo-tion.

It was as though the 'volume' of external 'other' had drowned out my own tune, as though these other influences all had a stronger pattern than my own and my own faded so far into the background as to seem not pres-ent at all. I may as well have been part of the wind or the water at that mo-ment. In fact, when I was older I found that at these times my breathing became extremely shallow and slow and my heart rate probably like that of someone in deep sleep, as though I actually continued to exist physi-cally only in a minimal way at these times. As I got older and more able to escape these states of involuntary resonance (sometimes if shocked out of them) the physical effect was like throwing cold water on someone in deep sleep and it really felt like 'coming back'.

I could resonate with the cat and spent hours laying in front of it, mak-ing no physical contact with it. I could resonate with the tree in the park and feel myself merge with its size, its stability, its calm and its flow. I could resonate with objects that had come from people and these carried a 'feel' not just of the object itself but of the person the object had spent time with; like an imprint left upon it, coexisting, yet unmuddied with the feel of the object itself, like simultaneously, yet discrete, existing systems.

On the level of 'will', 'I' was not only sensing the feel of these things but mapping them out in a sort of symbiotic physical merging with their energy. As an adult I'd once been walking at night in silence together with someone 'like me' when I felt as though some sort of non-wind wind had blown straight through me and all my hair stood up on end. It happened to him at the same time and we both stopped and stared at each other. He had asked me 'are you real?' and said it had felt like I'd just walked through him. At the time, I was in an hypnotic state and I had to scan my body to see that I actually had one. Perhaps this was what I'd had with objects but, unlike him, they'd been unable to tell me how they experienced my non-consciously-unintended out-of-body experiences.

It was through sensing that I established a depth of familiarity to which no amount of knowing or facts could add anything at all.

The knowing and interpretation of mind, by contrast, involved establishing familiarity from the outside-in and was a clumsy system based on observation. Sensing, by contrast, involved establishing familiarity from the inside-out and was a purer system that involved none of the distortions of constructed mind-self or discrimination between what the constructed mind-self considered worth knowing and what it did not.

The conscious mind is limited in its learning. It is slow and plodding and limited in the storage of information. On the other hand, the preconscious state in the absence of mind is indiscriminate. It doesn't filter incoming information in terms of personal or relative significance and takes in a wider scope of information than the conscious mind can. It takes it in at lightning speed and because it doesn't need to interpret that information it purely accumulates it and maps it. By my experience, the storage capacity of the preconscious state is, by comparison to the conscious mind, virtually infinite. The retrieval system, too, is different. Retrieval of preconsciously accumulated uninterpreted information is not through conscious voluntary attempts at accessing but through automatic triggering – as in a suggestive post-hypnotic state.

By the time I was three the system of sensing was more highly evolved in me than it would be in most people in a lifetime. The system of sensing was by then so finely tuned that I could sense patterns and shifts in patterns in almost anything within seconds and had also mapped out the patterns that these patterns led to. My system of sensing was as fully developed at three as the system of interpretation might have been for a so-called 'normal' child by the age of seven.

My system of sensing was so evolved that to people who relied on the slow and plodding system of interpretation, I appeared somehow to have precognition, as though I could tell what was about to happen before it happened and yet, when I attempted to rely on the interpretation of conscious thinking I was fallible, very fallible. Approached indirectly, my system functioned brilliantly. Approached directly, I was being prodded into a clutsy conscious mode.

At the age of three, unlike other children who by now relied on the system of interpretation, I could not consciously understand the meaning of words or sentences with any fluency (which is possibly one of the reasons the influence of social structures which would encourage redundancy of this system did not have the impact they might have had on another child).

In spite of an absence of interpretation, I could tell from the change in the pattern of a footstep or the slightest change in the sound of the vehicle pulling up outside the feel of the occurrences about to happen. I could tell in the shifting pattern of movements, from strong to erratic, to flowing, to extreme, the range of possibilities that would follow. I could tell from the sound with which a glass was put down, in response to the sound of another glass being put down, the basic feel or 'edges' of the interaction that would take place. I could tell from the incongruence between what was being portrayed and what I could sense, whether chaos was impending or fear and reactiveness was in the air.

Unlike someone relying on the system of interpretation, I didn't need to ask or question, not even mentally to myself. I didn't even need necessarily to look or to listen with consciousness, intent or focus. I didn't need to make conscious efforts to get to know. I wasn't 'psychic' in the common media sense of the word. It was merely that my system was quicker, less mechanical, less plodding than the system of interpretation. By comparison with those who relied on the system of interpretation, I was so slow that I wasn't even in the race. Yet, by my system, it was as though those who used interpretation were in another world.

The system of interpretation started up as gradually for me as a child as it probably does for a new-born. However, unlike a new-born, by the time that interpretation started happening I already had an established identity in terms of my first system; the system of sensing. So although I eventually and progressively took interpretation on board, the system of interpretation remained alien and disconnected to my self-identity and 'I' (in the sense of mind–will–identity) relied upon, trusted and identified with the system of sensing rather than the system of interpretation. To my inner self and what I later distinguished as my 'real self', sensing was flawless but interpretation could make so many mistakes and was unreliable.

Other people didn't seem to use sensing and I couldn't imagine how they couldn't (nor imagine how they could get by without it when it came so naturally and seemed the entire basis of trust). So I thought they were hiding the fact they could sense and I felt as though it were like a big joke being played on me which no one would let me in on. I found this excluding and scary and really it undermined trust. I knew they had the system of interpretation but I didn't know that, for many of them, this was all they had.

CHAPTER 5

The Mechanics of Sensing

People take in information through their senses. They look, listen, smell and touch and through this they take in information. They also take in information through movement and body feedback.

The taking in of information through the senses is about sensing and it is only when something is actually 'done' with this information, when it's processed, that the mind decisively addresses this information in a way specific to each individual. It is only when it goes beyond sensing to process what is sensed that the system of interpretation is at work. Without interpretation, all that is happening is accumulation, mapping and, perhaps, reflex.

There are different levels of interpretation. The first is the literal, the later stage goes beyond this to the significant. So, too, with sensing is there an earlier and later stage. Sensing through the physical body is a later form of non-physical sensing and one that starts up once one has actually established connection with one's body.

Body Connectedness

Before the body is even evolved properly, the brain already has the plans for how the body will evolve and for the functioning of different physically-based senses. This is the process of our in-carnation in the physical sense of the word (nothing at all to do with getting into flowers).

I suspect it is here, at this very early stage before the body is even fully formed and before the senses have become physically-based senses, that non-physical senses are at work. It is interesting that Webster's dictionary defines the word incarnation not just as 'embodiment in flesh' but also as 'to put an idea into concrete form' and it is true that we are born into our bodies before being born into the world and perhaps our conception is more than just an act of biochemistry. Perhaps our conception is a free floating idea of our potential existence brought eventually into concrete form. Certainly, spiritualists would insist that people can have sex but for a life to be conceived and continue fully into its (next) incarnation the energy form that will be that life has been drawn to or willed existence in that particular form. In this sense it is perhaps not that we have been conceived by our parents but that we conceived of our own potential existence which was drawn or willed into physical concrete form. It is not so much that we are born as that we have various stages of birth. Birth is not just the breaking of the surface as something emerges from the depths. Like death, birth has many stages and each is a birth in itself. Birth is also each leg of the journey from those depths of non-existence into gradual more fully expressed existence. It is in the nearing to that breaking of the surface and the stages of life after breaking that surface and walking on solid ground through life. Some of us are born before our physical birth, some of us take a long time after birth to be born fully into our bodies, our minds, our emotions. For some of us it may be as though we are undecided about commitment to our own existence or its continuation. Our growth, physically, mentally, emotionally, spiritually may become stunted, distorted, diverted, temporarily or longer term as life and death forces within us fight it out – as our will remains uncertain, indecisive, fluctuating or frozen.

In this early stage, without even conscious 'knowing' having come to life, that there is perhaps still the sensing of patterns and a resonance. As our conception becomes more and more concrete, we may come into contact with the environment in some progressively more physical form, if only through the mother's own patterns and shifts in pattern. It is in this time that responses, if any, may be selflessly echo-practic (in action) and echo-lalic (in sound), mirroring without alteration, without mind, that which the senses have accumulated as yet without interpretation. First we are born into the means and then refine the way those means are used, progressively with will before being taken over by mind.

With time, not only the body evolves, but also a perceptual sense of body connectedness and even before one is born, the senses have generally become physically-based. Most babies are born alert to the world with eyes that not only see but actively attempt to look and explore, ears that not only hear but actively attempt to listen, hands that not only feel but attempt to reach and a body that can not only move but that attempts to move with intention.

Occasionally, though, there are those who for one reason or other seem unaware and unresponsive, in spite of having functional sight, functional hearing and a functional sense of touch. I've seen this as being born unborn or born only partially born. Some spiritualists have referred to the same thing as being not yet fully incarnated. Will may give up on the physical form, its inherited weaknesses becoming exaggerated in their gradual degeneration as the will fails to adhere to the body. For most this wouldn't happen until an older age but certainly it has happened in even the youngest of lives, sometimes for observable reasons attributable to environment, sometimes perhaps for spiritual reasons completely unconnected with the environment. It may be that some may have taken all they had willed from this particular life form, regardless of the wants of mind.

The inability or delay in getting incarnated into mind may be that information processing is inefficient, perhaps because of circulation, auto-immune or metabolic problems. These may disturb the synthesis of vitamins and minerals or the regulation of blood oxygen or glucose levels, any or all of which are essential to the efficient information processing necessary to consistent interpretation. Without consistent interpretation, information overload may happen, giving a person the constant experience that the mechanics of interpretation are a source of discomfort to be avoided and this can become the nest in which an identification with the system of sensing is nurtured at the same time as a sort of anti-identification (a rejection) with the system of interpretation may start to evolve. It is also, however, possible that the very reason these cognitive mechanics fail to thrive as they should may be that will is not strongly committed enough to fight for the comprehension and awareness these mechanics might otherwise give. An aversion to being affected by this may lead to a poor development of areas of the brain and hormone system responsible for the experience of emotion and capacity to manage it. Just as the muscle tone and exercise capacity of healthy legs, not used, will waste without the drive to use them, the development of cognition, or even emotion may well be the same. Why, for example, in stroke victims who lose certain areas of cognitive function are so many able to redevelop skills or through will encourage other unaffected areas to take over these skills even at quite an advanced physical age, yet many who have not lost these skills but failed to be driven to develop them, have not done the same. There are certainly also those completely lacking in such will who acquire it later, making the same incredible advances.

It may not merely be that will loses connection because the environment has destroyed or diminished it. The system of interpretation may be abandoned for other reasons, the roots of which may lie in a past long before the person ever set foot on the ground in this lived life.

The will is a primitive and yet highly acute creature which carries sense-memories long before mind. It may be that a will which carries sense-memories of a time of freedom before the imposed confinement of body-groundedness, mind and interpretation, may have an instinctive aversion to graciously welcoming the onset of the system of interpretation or affect. An indecisive will may have been simultaneously drawn fiercely to life and avoidance of it. If the result were to be information processing problems which further justified the rejection not only of a stifling system but of an inconsistent and uncomfortable one, then spiritual progress in that particular expressed life form would be fairly restricted.

Those who haven't got fully into their bodies may still be 'there' in some earlier form, like someone who has fallen down a few rungs of the ladder but is still holding on a few rungs down. Perhaps babies who become children and adults who don't use their functional physically-based senses, may still be using non-physical senses from an earlier developmental stage. In other words, physical development may have continued but certain aspects of neurological or cognitive development may have remained or be delayed at an earlier stage.

These born unborn people often outgrow this at least to some extent and are called late developers or people with developmental differences or even developmentally disabled. But eventually, most do start to use their senses as others do even though the accumulated developmental delay may take many years to overcome (depending on the ferocity of the following rate of development). For example, Einstein and Mozart didn't speak till they were around four or five years old. Van Gogh was thought to have been affected developmentally. I personally have known two people who didn't have functional speech or develop social skills until they were twelve years old. One is now a musical genius with a pilot's licence and the other has a university degree in child development, teaches religious instruction and is a public speaker. It is not so much that the minds of these people may not want to develop – and some fiercely want this mentally – but if their will was opposed to the wants of mind, for whatever reason, the rate of development would be slower, less dynamic than it otherwise would be. There are many reasons for this, lack of trust emotionally even though the mind is unaware of trust as an issue, strongly sensing the harshness or impurity of the world in spite of not experiencing this with mind, feeling too vulnerable and exposed to dare expression in spite of having an established façade to hide behind, lack of confidence to express oneself clearly in a false world in spite of mind's commitment to the socially acceptable performance of mock self-expression.

Those who appear not to seek to make sense of their environment may not necessarily be 'retarded', disturbed, crazy or sensorily impaired, but may, in spite of not using the same system everyone else uses, still have one of their own. They may, in spite of apparent delayed development, actually continue to use a system that others have left behind very much earlier.

I began using non-physical senses to make sense of my environment. I could see but it did not naturally occur to me to look. It didn't naturally occur to me because I experienced no need to look.

Nothing could shock me because no interpretation was happening, no judgement and no thought. I appeared to stare into space and stare through things, like someone asleep with their eyes open, similar to a less grotesque version of a zombie. Though I was certainly not the living dead, it probably wouldn't be too incorrect to say that in some ways I was the 'born unborn'.

I could hear but had no need to listen and appeared to be deaf (and was tested for deafness at the age of two and again at the age of nine). In response to sudden loud noises, there was no response, not because I was deaf, for I could certainly hear sound and perhaps even more sound and more clearly than most people, but because I had no capacity to process sound, to interpret it and make the normally instinctual physical connections to respond to it.

I could feel but had no need of touch and appeared unable to feel pain. I could feel physical sensations but they were slow to register and were floaty and without distinct location or meaning or even a developed sense of whether they were internal or external to me. There was no response because the information, though perceived, remained unprocessed and uninterpreted.

I was somewhere between three and five when my body called me. It wasn't like it phoned me up or anything, it was just that it started to make its presence felt as though nagging me to listen to it and respond to it. At first, I tuned out this foreign invasion as was natural and instinctive to do with things that gave the feel of robbing one of control. Later, I tried to escape the sensed entrapment of physical connectedness, first spiritually by getting out of it and later physically by trying to pull it off from its suffocation of the me inside, slapping at it, punching it and later trying – physically – to run from it but the damn thing just came after me. As far as I was concerned, my body was welcome as a sensory tool, but as a body with something of a competing will of its own, it was like a leech that happened to be there by coincidence but wouldn't take the hint and couldn't be gotten rid of. It was my first known enemy.

CHAPTER 6

In Resonance

My body never did get the message but, eventually, some part of me did get a sense of who was in charge and my senses gradually became physically-based ones by the time I was three or four years old. As this happened, responsiveness did start up but it was the involuntary and indiscriminate accumulation and meaningless mirrored replay of the sounds and actions of others, without consciousness, without choice, without intention, without mind.

By this age, other children had a firm grip and identification with the system of interpretation and would have been searching for words or actions to express sensations or achieve the satisfaction of wants. I was still living by the system of sensing in which the whole concept of directing my environment hadn't yet been born.

Resonance with Objects

I moved from sensing through 'becoming one' with matter ('resonance') to using touch. Instead of merely 'taking on' the things around me in a sort of merging, I now began reaching out to them physically as separate entities.

My developmental condition affected how I processed sensory information. I wasn't able to filter incoming information properly so I was being sensorily flooded by it. The capacity to filter information requires some progressively accumulated sense of relative and personal significance and it is from this development of hierarchy that I think a sort of meta-self, some sort of psuedo-self or false self, is gradually born from mind.

Without this filtering, I was flooded and this led to a range of involuntary adaptations, one of which I call being 'mono'.

What being mono meant was that even though I'd progressed beyond mere mergence with things in my environment, I still had big restrictions in being able to process information produced from the outside and the inside at the same time. This meant that I could feel the texture of the wood, for example, but in taking the action physically to do so I would have no sense of my own hand. I could also switch channels and feel my own hand but would lose sensation of what my hand was in contact with. This also applied to my own body parts. If I touched my own face with my hand, I could feel the texture of my face *or* the effect upon my hand, but not both at the same time. I was either in a constant state of jolting perceptual shifts or I remained on one sensory channel or the other. It became far more natural to me to explore the textures of things using physical-based senses, but without being able to process my own body sensations in relation to these textures it was still, perceptually, as though either 'I' did not exist and other things did or they existed and 'I' did not.

Perhaps it was this very perceptual condition, this 'mono' state, that stopped my original non-physically based sensing from becoming a redundant system as it might have with anyone else who had more usual perceptual development. It could, however, be argued the other way. Perhaps, having lived for at least three years strongly exercising the use of non-physically based senses that required no simultaneous sense of 'self' and 'other', the various brain connections necessary for this perceptual development didn't happen and were perhaps even replaced by other functions.

To resonate with an object or surface takes no trying. Trying is an act of mind and mind is consciousness, firmly consciousness, and this is to have a conscious 'sense of self'. To merge with an object is to become it and one cannot do that with an intact sense of separate simultaneous existence.

When one has a conscious sense of self, there is always separateness from 'other' and always separability. When one has a conscious sense of self, one filters information and interprets sensory experience and whilst this builds the capacity to filter information, it also begins to limit how we perceive something external to ourselves. We can no longer take it in exactly as it is. Instead, this earlier mapping of relative and personal significance builds a cognitive net and information is taken in in terms of how we conceive of it based upon an accumulated and interpreted bunch of information.

Without a simultaneous sense of 'self' and 'other', one still has personal experiences but one does not build a cohesive scheme of interpreted experience through which new information is filtered and by which it is then interpreted beyond pure sensory (and sensual) experience.

To resonate with a surface or object and merge with it requires no conscious selection and no conscious interest or curiosity. Selection, interest and curiosity are acts of the mind. When you resonate with an object or surface it is not so much that you have reached out for that object or surface but that it has, somehow, reached into you.

Some children and adults have their senses (not to be confused with the mind) sharply awake. Sometimes these people are too sharply awake really to cope with life within conventional social structures. This is because conventional social structures require a mind to be developed to a degree capable of adequately processing the incoming information.

This sensory sharpness might be there for all sorts of reasons, including genetically inherited or acquired biochemical ones. Children and adults with the developmental condition Attention Deficit Disorder (ADD – often associated with a food intolerance to Salicylate and Phenol, particularly found in food additives and sugar) often have little choice regarding the bombardment of 'other' through their senses. Unable to filter out unwanted, or unnecessary information adequately, people with ADD are 'grabbed' by sensory experiences that come to them rather than the other way around. It is probably no coincidence that people with ADD often have considerable difficulty holding onto a thought or carrying out a complex, decisive and intentional action.

Even emotional connection or symbolism doesn't figure in the 'call' of these things, this sense of 'other' that jumps in. Experiences of resonance may be disciplined but they don't start that way. They start out (and probably almost always remain) entirely indiscriminate.

Yet, for this resonance to be possible don't we require some inherent map within us? Don't we need some physical-based experience that would map within us the sense of hugeness or tinyness, the sense of something being paper-thin or light or heavy or substantial, or the sense of something able to give way without effort or be unable to be budged? If not, how can we sense experiences we have no concept for? The answer is that we require concepts in order to interpret and understand but we do not require concepts in order to sense or experience. It is through the *interpretation* of what we sense or experience that concepts evolve.

Resonance and People

One could ask, what is the experience of merging, of resonance, worth if there is none of the reflection or consciousness that comes with bringing a conscious simultaneous sense of self to the experience?

Certainly, I cannot talk of these times as 'deep experiences' in the usual cognitive sense of the phrase and yet these experiences remain the deepest experiences possible. Perhaps only in death will I ever again know what it is to lose myself so wholly in the experience of something 'other', without sense of time or space, with no past, and no future and no here. There is no deeper experience than the total encapsulation of self within an experience until one *is* indistinguishable from the experience. It is like knowing 'God'.

Ask those who have ever flown, like butterflies, into the consuming flame of a deep and burning love with an insatiable hunger to merge. Those who've been there, ask yourselves, merge with what? Those who would speak of a new existence, of becoming one, might then ask, why is it then that in the rare instances that that merging is wholly known, even glimpsed, does it suddenly feel as if 'selfhood' may well be extinguished in the process? Perhaps it is not that one's selfhood becomes extinguished but that one's separateness, one's separability, becomes extinguished. Perhaps it is merely that what the mind considers its 'selfhood' hangs upon the experience of its own individuality and separateness.

I had always felt that such big emotions were the threat of death, the loss of a selfhood I'd fought so hard to attain and hold. Yet I, too, am drawn like that butterfly to the flame that is love. Is it that the mergence of 'in love' is the only force strong enough to overthrow the mind's sense of 'selfhood' and that in this death of mind our real inner self is born (or reborn) and freed from the weight of the false self-baggage and control and structuring of mind and freed also from the vulnerability of aloneness that is inherent in this separateness?

Is this why, in spite of gripping life, death, too, can be a freedom when we are ready to let go of the mind's selfhood that we associate with our ailing, decaying, ageing bodies? Yet, our culture is geared towards fear of death and dying and geared, simultaneously, to toying with it.

Perhaps the greatest struggle humans have with themselves and each other is the juggling of that balance between the tides of self and other. Perhaps an integrated and simultaneous sense of both is something impermanent and constantly fluctuating, subject to all sorts of biochemical shifts and Yin-Yang imbalances.

Human words are fickle. What, for example, is 'love'? Love is different things to different people. There is the mind-love that one tries for and works on which has to do with compatibility, familiarity and choice. This love brings with it a sense of self-government and self-control. This love is a meeting and it can be powerful in one's utter commitment to it.

There is also love that one finds in oneself without choice, like a pin to a magnet. Here, compatibility is not an issue, familiarity is redundant and choice is over-ridden. Here, there is no self-government of mind and no 'self-control'. This second type of love is not a meeting, it is a merging and it is addictive and powerful.

Some who have only known the first type of love have desperately wished to know the second. There are those who constantly find themselves swept up in tidal waves, merging, only to resurface, disoriented. Some of these people spend their lives wishing for a love with 'self-control' and watching cautiously for the next oncoming tidal wave in a futile attempt to control or hide from it.

The mergence I had with objects, I had also with certain people. I would call this an intense, uncontrollable empathy.

Many people confuse empathy with sympathy. Sympathy is almost the antithesis of empathy. Sympathy involves a simultaneous sense of self and other. Empathy involves feeling for the person deeply *as though you were that person*.

Walking through the supermarket, I physically felt the pain when someone banged themselves. Around someone with a broken leg, I felt their pain in my leg. The prickles or shivers would get me when I stood too close to someone without walls, as though their energy was affecting me. I could feel when people had real connected emotional pain whether they displayed it or not and I could feel when they were putting it on, when the display had no connection to the energy it was meant to come from.

When I felt their pain, I felt it within me and connection to my own feelings at the time simply switched off as though some frequency had interfered with my aerial. In the same way, the pain of an animal or even the distress of a tree can be sensed, whether physical or spiritual-emotional (not to be confused with a display of the mind's assumption of an expected or advantageous, yet mind-convinced, pseudo-emotion).

Mergence takes many forms. The magnetic attraction of 'in love' is just one of those forms, but the one many people seek.

Some people merged with me in a very different way. There were those who walked around within invisible walls; I could feel their walls no matter how polite or smiling or close they tried to appear (and wished to be). I resonated not with what was on the surface, but with the reality, taking on their walls as though they were my own. The more they hid their own walls, the more sharply I sensed them.

Some people, however, could capture me emotionally without trying. Merely to be touched by them or looked at could overwhelm me with feelings, sweeping my selfhood away as easily as cobwebs with a duster. With objects, this felt enclosed, taken in, warm and insular. With humans, this felt out of control and frightening. The lightning speed and enormity with which the 'self-connectedness' of mind gets washed away by such tidal waves felt like the threat of death (and it was the death of the mind's 'selfhood'). Though it is only such death for a short time, in the timeless void of the unalterable forever of the present this can only be sensed as the threat of death. Statements like, 'my heart skipped a beat', 'I almost died', and 'lost in love' may be expressing a reality that over time has got lost in the commonality of the phrases.

As a young child, people would enter my room and sometimes, without even looking, I'd merge with them and my sense of 'entity', perhaps the energy I identified as 'mine', left the room as them when they left again. When my body called me back, it was as though I'd had a sharp perceptual shift. It was as if I was surprised to find myself back with my own body.

Some people wish for such things and some people fear them. Those who wish for such things often wish with a greed and a negativity, an 'evil', that is born of fear and inadequacy and a desire to control others.

As a teenager, certain people found my ways attractive for the wrong reasons and I learned that what I experienced was dangerous. Later, I learned, it was not dangerous. I learned that it was not dangerous because as much as these sort of people might wish for these 'abilities' for their power, and even self-delude themselves they have them within their control, in my experience it is a fact that these people have too much mind-false self, too much conscious awareness and too much directed mind-want for these experiences to happen for them.

Those who fear such experiences should have no reason to fear. Those to whom these things happen are generally devoid of the sort of mind-false self and directed conscious awareness that would allow them to use these ways to hurt or harm or take from anyone. If there are any victims here, it is the person who finds time, space, body connectedness and connection to expressed mind-selfhood constantly disrupted by the bombardment of 'other'. Given the choice, most who have these ways would probably choose an easier and more consistent life without them.

Resonance and Places

One can stand in a wind and feel if it is a warm wind or a cold wind, a strong wind or a gentle wind. The wind is like an instrument with a limited number of notes. The resonance of a room or a place, is an intangible wind. It is an instrument with an unlimited number of notes.

Even with your eyes closed, a warm room can have a cold 'feel' to it. A room with opened windows can have a tight 'feel' to it. Without hearing a sound or seeing a thing, even standing somewhere outdoors with the wind blowing, there can be an enclosed and claustrophobic 'feel' to the place one is presently standing quite independent of your own thoughts and emotions at the time.

Just as the prickles and shivers would get me in resonance with some people, so too would they sometimes get me in resonance with certain places. Perhaps it is that just as people absorb the impact of experience, so too do places absorb the ever changing energy of the experiences that happen there. Sometimes, when the experience of time is not constant or linear, perhaps it is even possible to sense a lingering 'feel' to a place just as one might smell a lingering smell on the carpet from a beer-swilling party the year before or experience the lingering 'touch print' of a handshake that has already left a few seconds ago.

For me, this was the non-physically based sensing of places before I came to rely on physically-based senses. Some people call such things 'psychic' or 'clairvoyant' as though these things belong to 'special people'. I think those are terms born of ignorance that may sometimes do more harm than good and play into the hands of those who'd seek power and status by considering themselves somehow spectacular and above others.

Dogs and cats and horses have this sensing and can often sense the feel of a person or place. What is it then about the training of humans that they lose such a natural capacity? Perhaps another question is, in a society so geared towards power and status, what use would such a skill be if not to add to these things?

Non-physically based sensing, though it requires a body, probably mostly uses what might be called 'spirit' and it is my feeling that this is what eventually evolves into what people know as emotion.

People can learn to display mind-driven, pseudo-emotions and defend them as though they are real. In some people, mind has come to rule so much that felt emotion becomes redundant, replaced by the performance of pseudo-emotions. In others, emotion is at the heart of a still existent spirituality. The movement from non-physically based sensing to physically-based sensing is essentially a movement from reliance upon spirit and emotion to reliance upon the integration of spirit and body.

Physically-Based Sensing and Sensuality

Most people interpret using their eyes and ears, primarily. Yet, I don't believe we start out this way.

When I moved beyond reliance on non-physically based sensing, I had not yet developed the cognition necessary to interpret information through my eyes and ears at the lightning speed with which it was coming in. It just flooded in as a load of meaningless impressions. I began to 'get to know' my environment, not through interpretation, but through physically-based sensing and, for that, I began primarily through touch.

I began feeling textures and surfaces in my mouth, under my hands, on my cheek and through my (insistently) bare feet; shiny smooth surfaces, solid and cold surfaces, scratchy and rough surfaces, boingy surfaces that bounced back when touched, grainy surfaces and brittle crackling surfaces. Through touch, I came to know size and form and certain textures became 'friends' and special places to visit.

I developed physically-based mapping which involved knowing things not through their visual shape but through their shape experienced through my own physical movement. So, for example, if I felt a glass with my hands or gripped in my teeth, my concept of that glass had nothing to do with the word 'glass' or with how it looked or what it was used for, it had to do with the pattern of movement involved in feeling its form.

Later, I mapped objects through tapping them to produce sound and these objects were then known by their sound. In spite of seeing the object, I would always tap it to test its nature. Visual recognition remained a fragmented, poorly sequenced, relatively untrustworthy and meaningless system for a long time as did the interpretation of spoken language.

I also knew rooms by sound and by movement. I knew a room's familiarity by the amount of steps used to cross it and the sonics of the room. This meant I made special repetitive or sudden testing noises in certain rooms and this confirmed the familiarity of a room or its similarity to other rooms.

Later, smell and the way an object gave way when bitten became means of testing the familiarity of objects, places and even people. All of these things were gateways to grasping the experience of the existence of something outside of oneself.

Mine was a situation not unlike that of the deaf-blind. Unable to filter incoming information and being flooded with information at a rate I could not process in the context in which it happened, I was left meaning deaf and meaning blind as well as context deaf and context blind. Sometimes a sensory experience had no interpretation at all, leaving me in the sensory, struggling for the literal. At others it had literal meaning but had no significance.

I perceived sound and visual information directly and consciously only at the cost of its cohesion. I could interpret the part but lost the whole. I saw the nose but lost the face, saw the hand but continued to see the body but would not know what it was except piece by piece. I'd get the intonation but lose the meaning of the words or get the meaning of the words but only at the cost of tuning out the intonation, as though independent of the words.

The conscious mind, however, is not the only way of taking things in. The preconscious state takes things in, not directly, but indirectly. Using peripheral perception, we accumulate all the knowing we aren't always aware we are taking in. Taking things in indirectly, peripherally, the fragmentation didn't happen; things were more cohesive, they retained context. Yet the mind-jolting senses of direct vision and direct hearing could not be consistently relied upon as meaningful primary senses. In spite of this, I didn't remain under-developed, so much as I became differently developed. Like the deaf-blind, I used other systems more fully than most would ever develop them.

The Experience of Social

As someone previously reliant on resonance and non-physical sensing, the experience of 'social' was something I had been starved of. Without a simultaneous sense of oneself and what is external, there is no firm concept of 'social' nor even realisation of 'aloneness'. These experiences are such a part of shared human experience and the driving force that motivates people to physically seek out company. Without being able to hold onto these driving forces, the behaviour which was meant to stem from them – that of treating people consistently as people rather than as sensory objects – was at best slippery and at worst absent.

This is the state most people attribute to animals. They see humans as having progressed beyond this state, from the sensory and the sensual to the interpretive; a movement from body to mind.

Sensing the Nature of a Person

People generally 'get to know' people. That is how they build up a picture of that person's nature.

This is a knowing of the conscious mind. It involves analysis and comparison and learning. It involves judgement. It involves interpretation. It involves no feedback of one's own feelings to test the validity of this knowing. It stems from senses but moves beyond it, using sensing as a tool but then leaving it behind.

The mind develops as information is accumulated and used in the interpretation of new information. We are born with the capacity for developing a mind but until we have accumulated enough information and before our brain has mastered the mechanics of synthesizing this information in a way that enables it to use it in the interpretation of new information, we have brains but our minds are not developed.

Before people have developed a system of interpretation, they still have some form of self feedback. Their feelings tell them something about the sameness or difference between themselves and another person – whether there is congruence or incongruence, whether the presence of the other person causes a sense of exclusion by virtue of a sensed threat or repelling force or whether it causes a sense of inclusion by virtue of some sensed accepting or attracting force. This is instinct and animals have it and they sense it about people regardless of who a person thinks they are or tries to be. It is that sensed something that makes the hairs stand up on your arms or makes you shiver or pull away or makes you grimace or tense up in spite of no obvious physically perceivable sign of threat.

Some animals seem to 'know' before they even smell another creature. I believe that what they sense is the congruence of a capacity for resonance with what is sensed, the lack of it or the incongruence of sensed dissonance. I believe they sense what I came to call in human words, 'edges'.

Edges

Fluffy edged people make me squirm like a worm.
They cause me 'lemons', make me squidgy.
I respond like they have germs.

Some are gentle, some are lovely.
Some are overwhelmingly bubbly.
Some are motherly, even smotherly.
Some are pillows feeling cuddly.

Hard edged people, you can lean on.
They don't strike out and they don't crumble.
They don't cause me indecision.
They provoke no mental jumble.

Some are logical, responsible,
credible and sensical.
Some are pillars of society.
Some are fully indispensable.

Sharp edged people, they are crisp.
They whip out, some are conniving.
Some have heavy ego baggage,
or have their real selves in hiding.

They can get you in a web
or set you up
or pin you down.
They can present themselves as friends,
or be sarcastic as they clown.

Brittle edged people, they are crumbly,
even efficient, they are fumbly.
Some are wishy, some are washy.
Some hide their 'brittle' within 'poshy'.

Some brittle edged people,
find the world a bit too much.
Some blame it easily on such and such.
Some run about in such a rush.
Some fall apart and some are mush.
Some get broken in societal crush.

Some people they have bits of each,
each hiding under one another,
where a lover is a monster,
or an angel, an impostor.

Some people, like some bits they find,
but do not like all the rest.
They sort what they find best,
then ignore or hate the rest.

With themselves, some people fight,
to correct or to put right,
to abandon or destroy within,
the little girl or boy within.

The demon or the angel,
they may slap or punch or strangle,
and never realise the tangle,
is their own.

I knew people by their 'edges'.

Fluffy edged people generally had a presence that was bubbly and warm. These were people who were emotionally expressive, allowing their emotions to flow freely and consistently.

These people seemed to drift or bounce along, caught up on various waves of emotion and basically not ruled by mind. These were people who were drawn to other people and there was a flow between them and others that seemed to sustain them like soul-food.

To be in their company was to be swept up by the human equivalent of a billowing cloud as it blew across the sky of life. Their free-flowing emotions, contagious in their effect, were not easy for me to handle as someone who feared emotion and being affected and out of control. Yet the presence of these people is so often so uplifting and devoid of the harshness and intensity of those ruled by mind that it was ironic that those I liked best seemed hardest to handle being near.

Hard edged people, by contrast, had reigns on emotion. They took control of it. Its flow was controlled and sometimes quite held in.

These were self-owning people, though not necessarily hard people in the usual sense of the description. Often these people were external and ruled by mind, interacting with others generally within defined structures and not wildly free-flowing. Yet these people could be caring, even intensely caring, but able to care with the practicality and planning of mind and the personal objectivity that sustains their foothold in their own reality and probably also their sanity.

Hard edged people were decisive people in whose company you could feel some certainty and predictability. Even if you, yourself, had no idea what was going to happen, these people usually had some idea.

Sharp edged people were unpredictable, their patterns often chaotic, staccato in their expression. These were reactive people, basically ruled by the defensive mind I call constructed-false self, rather than the logical-practical-decisive mind.

Sharp edged people could be highly charismatic and seemingly passionate. These were not self-owning people and generally depended highly on having something or someone to react to.

These people lived a reality where everything seemed to reflect back upon them and cause a reaction. This could misleadingly make them appear highly motivated in a very linear sense of the word but this is a very specific type of motivation and certainly very different from that of hard edged or fluffy edged people.

Sharp edged people could appear strong but, not being self-owning, theirs was a defensive version of strong and not the internal strength one associates with endurance or with knowing oneself.

I never felt able to relax in the company of sharp edged people and my life was already too chaotic to seek the entertainment value sometimes found in these sometimes quite dramatic people.

Crisp edged people (also-called scratchy edged people) were merely watered down sharp edged people.

These people appeared strong but it was more that they 'held themselves' together than that they possessed a true internal solidness of self. I never chose these people as my special people to be around. These were people I treaded around if possible.

Unlike crisp edged people, brittle edged people were those who had been fluffy edged people who had become damaged by life in some way. Brittle edged people were breakable, sometimes resulting in a mild defensive reactiveness but more often resulting in a turning inwards. I sometimes had deep empathy for fluffy edged people who had become brittle edged because I admired what they'd either once been or had the potential to be again if they swung fluffy rather than sharp. I could almost feel the damage that had turned them brittle edged.

Sometimes people were generally entirely one type of edge or another regardless of who they were with. Others changed from one type to another depending on company, as though, unlike objects, people become essentially fragmented or multiple in response to the complex structures and experiences of life. Certain others could bring to the fore a more recessive part of these people.

I've been in the company of those for whom alcohol or drugs or even the drug-like effects of food or chemical allergies/intolerance, brings different edges to the fore. My mother, for example, lived in the company of others essentially as what I sensed as a sharp edged person. Yet in the company of herself she was basically hard edged and when quite drunk she occasionally became brittle edged, showing basically a damaged fluffy edged person within her.

Affected severely by food and chemical intolerances, certain substances brought to the fore my hard edged side and yet others, equally, brought to the fore my fluffy edged side, and occasionally even a sharp edged side, leaving me swinging, often suddenly, between the logical, the sensual and the defensive-reactive.

Edges have nothing to do with actions. Hard edged people may be as likely as any fluffy edged person to coo over a baby in quiet gentle tones. A sharp edged person may be a sympathetic friend or counsellor. A hard edged person may be a highly expressive comedian or entertainer. A fluffy edged person may be a business-like accountant or a lawyer.

Behaviour can be driven from emotion or from mind. Behaviour can reflect a sort of constructed behaviour-self which has stemmed from the stored learning of the mind or it can reflect the inner self, the emotional self – one's edges.

Regardless of edges, people, all people, have an entire range of emotions, acquired mind-interests and mental and/or emotional motivations. Edges are found in pattern – not in the pattern of one action or expression but in the composite picture of a whole range of very different actions and expressions and people can also use stored overlaid patterns which have no connection to their inner self and contrast sharply with what would otherwise be a naturally flowing pattern.

The way a foot is placed on the floor in stepping will be different for people of different edges, regardless of whether each is tiptoeing, in a hurry, depressed, happy or whatever. Within any one person, the way the foot is placed on the floor will also be very different if a stored overlaid non-self pattern is used as opposed to when a step is used which is connected to inner self. The same is true of the way a glass or a plate put down on the table will express edges or the overlay and sell-out of them regardless of purpose or feeling at the time. Similarly, the pace and tone of all movement, gesture and sound expression will express edges regardless of intent or the image one attempts to project.

Edges are the 'be' beyond 'appear'. They are the truth beyond the façade. They are the essence beyond the overlay of acquired constructed pseudo-personality. Edges are the foundation of selfhood; its body without the clothes that either fit it or disguise it.

When a hard edged person crosses the room using non-stored, self-connected actions, I see and hear the self control born of self-ownership even in the absence of seriousness, purpose or intent. When that person reaches for something as their inner self or puts it down, I see and hear the same. When that person coughs, sneezes, laughs, cries, shrieks or speaks without stored overlays, I hear hard edges. When that person sits or stands or has facial expression or body language as their naturally flowing, non-acquired self, I see hard edges.

As themselves, the foot hits the floor with a firmness and surety even when the person is happy, relaxed or in a state of confusion. When the glass is picked up without stored action, even in a state of insecurity, the firmness, the self-ownership remains. When a hard edged person coughs or laughs without stored overlay, there is an inner instinctive control that comes through and a regularity and consistency to the sound; it is controlled, not consciously, but from within, in line with the edges which dominate in that person.

When a fluffy edged person's foot hits the floor without façade, it has a freedom that is devoid of control which marks it as a fluffy edged footfall and the same is true of other fluffy edged expression – voluntary or involuntary. Fluffy edged expression has a consistency but a consistency which speaks of a lack of reins upon the free-flow of expression through the body. These spirits aren't contained neatly and firmly within the body, as with hard edged people. Instead they seem sometimes to exude beyond it.

Sharp edged non-pseudo expression has a 'staccato' feel to it. The pace and tone of expression, regardless of mood or intent, has a marked inconsistency to it that gives a feel similar to a sharply prodding finger which comes out of the blue in the midst of a peaceful waltz. Expression, in the reins of the defensive mind, is also often out of synch by comparison with the free-flow of expression that comes with fluffy edges.

Animals, like humans, have edges and I suggest the possibility that in continual prolonged involvement with humans, animals, like humans, become more fragmented, more multiple in their edges and acquire more stored pseudo-expression (stored non-self expression) than they would if they lived purely around wild animals.

I would suggest that trees have edges and it may even follow that these edges may be affected quite differently when dependent on the involvement (or 'care') of humans from how they might be when independent of this involvement. Perhaps this is what people once described as tree spirits and I certainly have also felt the edge to a certain wind or tide.

I've met hard edged pups and fluffy edged dogs. I've met a hard edged cockatoo, a sharp edged cat and had a brittle edged horse. I had two sheep who were sisters, one fluffy edged and one hard edged (who got along well) and two pigs, one fluffy edged and the other sharp edged (where the sharp edged one gave the fluffy edged one hell). I've met two trees I sensed as hard edged (among two of the most memorable of my tree friends). There have also been many trees, particularly some potted ones, which I sensed as devoid or weak in their edges. One could speculate whether 'inhumane' or 'dehumanising' treatment of any living entity has the capacity to weaken its spirit and perhaps that's what edges are – a sensing of the spirit or relationship of energy to its boundaries, rather than an acquaintance with the social construction of acquired mind.

Edges have nothing at all to do with interpretation. You can't sense edges with your conscious mind. You map them with your preconscious mind and, if you are lucky enough to have good dream recall, be a persistent daydreamer or be able to tune in to your own tuning out, then you might actually have the blessing of being able to visit consciously the unknown knowing of your preconscious mind or at least allow its automatic expression to burst through.

Edges have nothing to do with *why* a person does what they do. They have only to do with a feel of *who* a person is. The feel of who a person is has nothing to do with *what* that person lives. Much of this may well have no connection at all to *who* that person is inside and many people themselves can be very shocked to find they are not actually who they had assumed they were or didn't actually feel what they expected or even mentally convinced themselves they felt.

Many people assume their *who* is their *what* and it's not, any more than their *who* is their *why*. Now you're probably really confused.

A person's predominant edges remain regardless of the WHAT a person does.

Socially, we are taught there are 'artistic types' and often fluffy edged people are drawn to 'arty lifestyles'. Yet if you take a look at art, it is produced by hard edged people, sharp edged people, brittle edged people as well as fluffy edged people. In fact, being the most freely expressive, fluffy edged people, though sometimes comfortable living an 'arty lifestyle', may actually be so expressively non-stifled that they don't *require* the release of art as much as some hard edged or sharp edged people might and it is that need which is so often the driving force which motivates people to be expressive through art.

Hard edged people may be more reliant on technique to the point that the self-expression they seek to set free is confined even in the art they produce. Sharp edged people, expressing some of their reactiveness through art may then even react to their own reactiveness objectified through art, putting down, hiding or destroying what they produced.

So edges don't dictate what one does so much as how one is more likely to do it. Edges are probably more likely to be seen in how someone holds a brush than in the art produced by the brush itself unless social learning has dictated the holding of the brush as well as the subject and style of the painting.

The fluffy edged lawyer, by instinct, may be more likely to deal in empathy unless trained out of allowing this to be freely expressed or trained into using another agreed-upon approach instead. The hard edged lawyer, by instinct, may be more likely to deal in logic and motive yet still appeal to understanding and yet may be trained to behave 'empathically'. The sharp edged lawyer, by instinct, may be more likely to use provocation and impact and yet be trained to be more passive. Social learning can unteach the expression of any instinct and can put it into a back seat. Yet though it can bury it and leave it to become unexercised, rusty and redundant, it cannot erase it and it is always recoverable from the cobwebby archives in which it was left. In recovering 'true self' there will always be benefits and penalties that will need weighing up with a self-honest and open mind. To weigh it up with mind alone, or in terms of the small picture within the present structures only, and expect to recover true self, may be like looking for Avalon.

People who live by interpretation alone live by mind and in this realm everything has a point even if that point is yet to be discovered or made up. For people who live by mind the obvious question might be, what's the point of edges or soul? What could these things possibly tell us?

Many people who live by mind alone doubt there is a soul. Many are content to trust mind alone and think all their acquired patterns speak of their 'real self', their 'felt emotions'. They may be unable to tell a pseudo-emotion or a pseudo-experience from a real one. Tuned out to real emotion or inner experience they may believe that the thought which stems from a complexity of stored learning is dialogue with soul and be unable to see beyond the appear. They may be utterly convinced of their own self-delusion and confuse knowing their stored learning and what scenes they buy into with knowing themselves.

Edges told me who my edges were compatible with; a kind of soul dialogue that is based on feel, not on thought. Edges gave me some 'feel picture' of who different people were; a picture that sustains itself over time regardless of life changes, appearances, façades. Relying on edges, there were special people who knew me also by my edges and for them I was the person who could drop in and out of their lives over years and every time I walked back in the door, things took up from where they left off. Even if years had passed, edges didn't change even if the behaviour and ever changing happenings of lives had.

When I dropped back into the lives of sensing people, they too took up exactly where things left off. When I dropped back into the lives of people who were non-sensing people (who relied on interpretation rather than sensing) they seemed somehow surprised, even shocked, that I'd assume the relationship to be the same when they'd 'been through so much' since I last saw them or felt they'd 'changed'. For me, the core of who a person was never changed even though certain people, places, happenings can shift someone from their own edges, even leaving them in resonance with the edges of someone, something or somewhere else. Their way of relating to me may have changed, the things they did with their time, the way they dressed, the people they saw, the music they listened to, their thinking, all changed. Yet the people – their sensed edges – never changed.

I lived in a world of constructed egos and minds and bodies, of lives and trends. But all I saw were souls and everything else was transient background information which I got trained to take account of long after other people had acquired the mental capacity to take account of it instantly, as foreground.

CHAPTER 7

Giving Self a Chance to Answer

Many people confuse sensing with thinking. They may say, 'I sense all is not as it seems here' and actually mean 'I (mentally) suspect all is not as it seems here'.

Sensing comes from a time before mind. It has nothing to do with suspicion. Suspicion comes from learning, learning which has come from the interpretation and storage of interaction patterns.

Sensing is much more basic. When a new-born calf staggers to its feet for the first time, or a cat delivers and cleans its first litter of kittens, it doesn't suspect that if it does X then Y will follow. It just follows what its instinct tells it, a gut feeling, something sensed before the mental learning of everyday life even starts. People have this too but we've become convinced we need to learn everything with mind. We've made mind our God and have little faith in the sensing that things would come naturally. Yet without being taught, we'd still make sound patterns; given just two of us, we'd probably still form some type of communication system that vaguely resembled language even if it wasn't a pre-existing one. We'd still, like the new-born calf, explore our legs and arms, learn to walk and reach and manipulate objects. We'd still explore the focus point of smells and taste them, eventually distinguishing the edible from the inedible. We'd still learn to distinguish between a comfortable and uncomfortable place to sleep and find shelter. We'd still be emotionally aroused by experiences and our emotions, at least on a sensory level, would be formed. Without being taught, we'd still absorb the sensory patterns of the world around us from which we'd later form more and more complex patterns of interpretation which gets called 'thought'.

Humans forget that all current learning started somewhere. Sometimes no one taught the teacher; some discoveries just happen, by chance or exploration and very often the best and most useful ones are totally unguided by rational thought and purely accidental. Some children and adults learn not because of teaching but in spite of it. People who've never been to school or been unable to make use of school have learned to read from the labels on products, to speak from TV jingles, and to understand social situations from novels. This is learning without being taught. Often when we teach, we think we are helping people to use their own thought processes when often we are only teaching them to use our own, not theirs. Outside of the 'teaching' situation, what appeared to be 'learned' gets dropped as the foreign and alienating little episode of non-self compliance it so often was. Perhaps some people don't have learning difficulties so much as they have difficulty holding on to and using baggage that doesn't feel like their own.

To sense that something is not as it seems has to do with an asymmetry between what 'appears' (and is able to be interpreted by mind) and what is sensed (which can only be felt through the body and confirmed through the emotions). When one senses no discrepancy between the appear and the be there is harmony within the self between body and mind in response to the experience. There is symmetry.

On the other hand, the 'appear' of an experience may be giving very clear and strong mental messages that something is not for you and yet the body may not respond in accordance with the way the mind conceives of the experience. The emotions may confirm that what the mind conceives as not for you is actually somehow 'meant to be'. A battle may then take place between emotions and mind as to which will rule action.

People can develop 'mock-emotions'. This is particularly where real felt emotions contradict what the mind expects a felt response to be or where the mind finds felt emotions inconvenient, uncomfortable or socially disadvantageous. Here the mind has total rule over the person. It has stored the displayed expression of the range of emotions and can drive the display of whatever emotion it expects should be there according to its interpretation of an experience. People can develop mock sadness, mock happiness, mock excitement, mock fear, mock guilt, mock shame, mock embarrassment, mock love. They can even display mock smiles, mock laughter and crocodile tears and, in the absence of real emotion, may be utterly convinced these are a hundred per cent real. People may do this for a whole range of reasons. They may be too emotionally sensitive and find emotions overwhelming or confusing. They may fear or feel uncomfortable with the loss of control which happens when emotions are felt. They may have been hurt by life when made vulnerable by being emotionally affected and now close out this invisible enemy. Or they may develop mock emotions simply because they've decided, consciously or unconsciously, that emotions and their effects have no place within their bought-into lifestyle.

People may function using mock emotions only in certain social situations or they may live like this in every regard. When someone acquires and adheres to an extensive and pervasive repertoire of mock-emotion and mock-expression, the person actually develops a pseudo-self. All of these are like invisible walls which close out or restrict the system of sensing and internal felt 'dialogue' with one's own soul (not to be confused with thought). One of the most tragic consequences of this is that these people not only go on to live performed lives as living corpses but they sometimes then become addictively driven to seek 'bigger', 'better', even 'more outrageous' experiences in a controlled and mentally applied attempt to evoke an emotional reaction. This is like tying up their soul in a straightjacket, gagging it, dehumanising it, devaluing it, ignoring it but visiting it every so often to stick it with a pin. The other tragedy about this is the fear, even terror, these people may experience when the straightjacketed true emotions finally break through (sometimes in the form of a partial or total emotional breakdown) and these are felt as foreign, alienating, invading, control-robbing. The greatest madness of this is that the 'natural' response is then to fight these off like the enemy.

Where the mind interprets information, the body senses the 'feel' of something, its pattern or the relative symmetry or asymmetry between 'appears' and 'be'. Those who know only reliance on mind as 'knowing' may ask, 'but how can I read what I am sensing and what it means and what I'm meant to do about it?'

The mind lives in a world of guarantees and demands them, perhaps because the clumsy learned system of interpretation *is* so hit and miss that as much as one may pride oneself on being clever, when faced with the unpredictable there is always something one doesn't know. If you truly want to listen to the system of sensing, give up your addiction to the necessity to confirm everything with mind. Give up the assumption that the knowing of the mind is the only knowing there is of any value. For even in a world which takes as natural the unnatural encouragement, reinforcement and reward for fragmentation, in their nature people are still essentially whole beings, not just heads, but bodies and emotions too. Here lies the sort of intimate and personal self-honesty that is called 'I feel' or 'I sense' which is equally as valuable as the 'knowing' of mind even if you can't hand it to any other person outside of yourself in written, testable form.

I have been in the grip of emotion without mind. I have known too what it is to let the mind's addiction to control roam free, straightjacketing inconvenient and uncomfortable emotions which would interrupt mind's structures and its addiction to seeking a world of guarantees. I have experienced the fool's achievement of calling façade 'self' and the terror of being reclaimed by the inner feeling self I'd abandoned, denied, defied and defiled. I learned the hard way that mind is not the god it claims to be. My mind strayed from my soul but it ultimately got dragged back to being the servant of the master it had sprung from in the first place. My soul, the capacity to sense, gave birth to my mind, not the other way around.

The mind is reckless to assume so arrogantly the right to meddle with a system it does not comprehend but has learned to assume it does (perhaps out of fear of vulnerability or impotence). To sense something, one has to tune into the body sensation the experience causes and read this as an attracting force or a repelling one undriven and uninfluenced by the 'wants', ideas or taboos of mind. The attracting force, one could call a positive feeling. The repelling force, one could call a negative feeling. But remember, mind is a labyrinth of self-deception, ever ready to call its vested interests something felt, natural, right...whatever will justify it getting what it seeks.

The mind may compel action towards something but this doesn't necessarily mean one is drawn to it on the level of sensing. Someone may sense an inner withdrawal from what he or she is attracted to regardless of how much the mind compels him or her toward it. Alternatively, the mind may compel action sharply away from something but this doesn't mean one is repelled by this on the level of sensing. One may sense an inner attraction towards what one's mind is repelled by.

All of this is pretty basic. It tells us the direction our urges are taking but it doesn't tell us what this means for us or what we are meant to do about it. The mind would have its share of answers to this and would gladly step in but our emotions may have their own things to say.

When there is asymmetry between mind and emotion, it is hard to go by one's expression. The mind can drive all sorts of unfelt utterances, facial expressions, postures and actions which it may firmly believe are felt but which are emotionally disconnected. But don't assume that real emotion is always on the side of felt urges either. Emotion is the realm of unknown knowing. It comes not from the plodding conscious mind but from the preconscious and subconscious mind with its infinite capacity for a range of connections that the mind could never keep up with. Yet, where thought can be accessed, real felt emotion cannot and can only be triggered in order to find out its response to a given situation.

If you are asked or ask yourself 'what do I think about this?' or 'is this good for me?', the mind will usually access all sorts of thought responses; 'well, I think this doesn't suit', 'I think I can't afford this', 'I think I don't need this', 'I think this would mess me up'. But if you were asked or mentally asked your emotions these same questions, your mind may answer on their behalf but your emotions would probably have no reply. They would probably have no reply because you are addressing them in a language they don't speak. The mind speaks in accessible thought and can answer questions. The emotions speak in evoked triggerable reaction and respond not to questions but to statements.

Think about Tommy who has taken some money from the jar. If you ask him, 'did you take the money from the jar?', then Tommy's mind may answer you with 'yes, I did', 'no, I didn't', 'it wasn't me', 'Joey took it', 'you always blame me' etc. Tommy's mind, for all sorts of reasons, may even convince itself that any one of these replies are true whether they are or are not. Say to Tommy, 'you took that money, didn't you?' and it will be the same since the question equally provides the room for all sorts of responses from mind.

Emotions require specific triggers. You either hit the nail on the head or you do not. Calmly and objectively (without inspiring any anxiety which makes the mind step in and take over) ask Tommy not to speak or say any word at all in response to what you are about to say. Then forget about asking and present, without any hint of doubt, the stated theoretical possibility, 'Tommy took the money' and wait without prejudgement (for any sensed or perceived prejudgement can trigger the mind to come to the defence). If Tommy's mind is not on red alert and Tommy's emotions know he did take the money, they'll speak up, not in words but through body.

If Tommy didn't feel he took the money, you would not have hit the right trigger and could state, in the same calm and objective way, 'Tommy didn't take the money' and his emotions would probably respond. This is what happens when the cheeky grin breaks through, when the face becomes flushed, when the nervous rash breaks out, when the nervous tic starts up, when the eyes twinkle. These are ways the emotions speak, not through words, but through body.

I've got a tic in my foot called 'my happy foot' which takes off when truth is hit upon, when I'm excited and sometimes when I'm anxious. It's something I can't easily do with conscious effort. It's an evoked thing. I used to have an exposure-related nervous rash which would break out and cover my chest and neck and I have a cheekiness in me that my twinkling eyes can never deny when I'm caught out. Basically, my emotions cannot lie and as much as mind may dictate to body to contain them, eventually they find their way out through the cracks regardless.

But people can read into things what they want to see in there. Needy people can attempt to evoke the exposure of emotional truths and when they don't see what they expected or wanted to see may tell themselves they saw it anyway. Angry or guilty or fearful people can do the same, seeking to justify their own feelings. Embarrassment can be taken to be confirmation. Wishful thinking or the thought one is capable of a deed may actually trigger an emotional confirmation of the doing of the deed itself whether it was done or not. The system of sensing is a thing of purity and vulnerability which should be respected. In the right hands, it can be a tool with which to free those who for one reason or another are effectively imprisoned within themselves.

CHAPTER 8

The Getting of 'Clever'

People are from the first, even before birth, capable of sensing. Our first wholly conscious experiences are through the body and it is the processed stimulation of the body that eventually awakens consciousness and the development of mind. So too, when one leaves the mind, such as when in a deep hypnotic state or coma, it is again through tuning back in to the body that one gradually re-awakens into conscious awareness, mind and the system of interpretation.

One is not born with the data base by which to interpret information but, unless something dramatic happens to effect sensory, perceptual or cognitive development, one is usually born with the capacity to make the connections necessary to build that data base and access it; capable of conscious awareness and of mind. For some people, this process will take longer than it will for others and in the meantime there is still the system of sensing.

For some, this process may be so significantly delayed that identity becomes formed before the system of sensing is developed enough to be relied upon. If this development is significantly delayed, a person may develop intense opposition to the apparent intrusion or challenge to established identity. When the system of interpretation finally begins to kick in and compete with the earlier system of sensing as the dominant system to govern action it could be experienced by some people not as the birth of selfhood but as the beginning of its death.

In my case, I remember this transition from the system of sensing into the system of interpretation began to happen not in the first days and weeks of life as is usual but at around three years old. It was not until around the age of ten that the system of interpretation (with much begrudgement) eventually came to be relied upon rather than merely put up with or tuned out. Even then, it was taken on, not as a first and primary 'language' but as a secondary one and much later as one of two equal but different 'primary' systems.

The data base we use in interpreting information is specific to the historical time and place into which we are born and develop. That data base is specific to the social and cultural structures and values around us and the way others respond to our gender, our age, our genetic inheritance or any acquired condition. We come into the world with some form of inherited software that is taken care of or not. We are usually formatted for the information we will be subject to depending on things like inheritance, handling and biochemistry, but the actual data gets inputted, directly and indirectly, whether we like it or not.

The system of interpretation uses a data base of patterns but also symbols. Some of those symbols correspond to facial expressions, postures, actions but also to ascribed culture-specific sound patterns that people call 'words'.

Most words do not relate in any direct way to sensory experiences. The word 'cat' says nothing of the sound that comes from the thing when stroked, the noise it makes or the tactile sensation felt when stroking it. I had developed two words for the sensory experience of 'cat'. One was 'foosh' which defined it by the sound made by your hand over the fur when stroking the creature. The other was 'brook' (with a rolled 'r') which defined it by the noise which came out of the creature when it was stroked.

The word 'concave' is used to describe the internal shape of a spherical object but it says nothing of the sensory experience. The word 'whoodely' does for if you run your hand quickly around the space within a spherical glass bowl you will hear (if your hearing is sensitive enough) something very much like 'whoodely'. If you asked me the name of something within the system of sensing I'd tell you to ask it. You wouldn't do so in words, you'd ask it through the interaction between it and your body and it will tell you its 'name'.

Mind and the System of Sensing

The system of sensing is of brain but not of mind. The realm of words and of curiosity are of mind. They are tools and mechanisms born of the system of interpretation and have no place within the system of sensing and are, in fact, its off switches.

It has been said that in order to tune in one must tune out, that real sensory awakening doesn't happen when the mind is alert but when it is off guard, in something of a more meditative state. It is there that mind stops interfering with interpretation, filtering out information by tuning in only to what it considers personally false self-significant. With the mind tuned out, one tunes in to pattern, having the feel of this wash over oneself, mapping it out without the discrimination of interpretation.

A cat, relaxing into being stroked, shows little conscious regard for whether it is being an imposition and the more wholly it gets swept up in its sensations, the less consciously aware it is. The opposite is also true and a human, geared toward mental alertness of the impact of their touch on another person may not, themselves, be fully able to experience the sensory nature of their own touch whilst living in the realm of mind rather than body (of which the brain is a part from which mind sprang).

The same may also be true of the loss of sensory pleasure which can happen when someone constantly asks you what you are feeling at the time of being touched because it may not so much be self-consciousness that then gets triggered as mind-consciousness. The mind becomes triggered in its role to start interpreting the words it's been highly trained to interpret and respond to. Sayings like 'stop worrying and just enjoy yourself' (or 'shut up and enjoy yourself') may speak of an intuitive understanding of the mechanics of sensing that people may have forgotten.

Sensory exploration is different from 'curiosity' but may look the same. What many people call 'curiosity' is an act of the mind which springs from a need for mind-knowledge or false self-reassurance. It is not that these people are curious to touch for the sensation itself but for the socially learned mental significance of that sensation. Sensory exploration, however, is not mental. It is more primitive and somehow beyond the mental. It is the following, not of mind, but of instinct.

Mind has come to replace so many things. Mind can conjure up pseudo-emotions, performing them as though they are real and in place of real feelings which the mind finds inconvenient, embarrassing or difficult to deal with.

Mind can call compulsion 'want' or 'like' when, if freed from the basis of the compulsion, the target of the compulsion may actually be something one is indifferent to, or even has an aversion to.

Mind can have pseudo-curiosity and pseudo-understanding, able to put on the performances that go with understanding that may not actually be there at the time but which the mind has socially learned is meant to be advantageous to portray.

Mind can have pseudo-expression, able to burble off a range of facial-expressions, postures, movements, phrases and conversations which it has learned bring acceptance, interest, present a certain image or stop one from being noticed.

Mind can have a constructed pseudo-personality based on social learning in place of the real one which may, by contrast be considered less impressive, more clumsy, less advantageous, and remain unexpressed.

Mind can have pseudo-body sensations according to learned ideas of what should be felt or how others would respond to one having certain sensations.

Mind can construct a pseudo-reality, overlaid so strongly over the existing reality that the existing reality, by contrast, may appear less interesting, less advantageous, less impressive, less structured, less easy to manage and may fade into the background, visited less and less until sometimes no longer visited at all, as though swallowed up by the pseudo-reality which outshone it.

Mind itself can become an internal reality, so compelling as to make the external reality redundant in terms of belonging and familiarity. Mind holds no keys to the system of sensing but it holds many keys with which to lock that system out.

Evolution

Sensing is one of the only things in life that involves no learning and yet, for those who lose the system of sensing, they may actively have to apply themselves to rediscovering it. The mind can learn through sensing and it may confuse interpretation with sensing and, in the absence of sensing, assume it to be such, but the mind itself doesn't learn to sense.

The mind does, however, learn how to interpret and as it comes to be the dominant system, it comes to dictate which senses to use over others and what sort of information is more worth taking in than other sorts of information. The mind learns to judge and discriminate and in that process we lose a certain freedom; the freedom to let life speak to us in its enormity and in its own language.

If the mind did not step in and begin to interpret and come to dictate which information was worth more than other information, we would potentially be less alike, perhaps even less what we all recognize as 'normal' or even 'human'.

If we did not develop the capacity to filter out sensory information, we'd probably blow all sorts of fuses in the information processing department of a mind which has only limited capacity to process incoming sensory information in an integrated way.

Without filtering out a certain degree of incoming sensory information, the slow working equipment of the conscious mind wouldn't be able to keep up with the pace and, unable to make the number and depth of connections it otherwise might with this information, the ways in which we then might communicate, relate, even think or feel, might be very markedly different to what most people think of as 'natural' or 'normal'.

Without developing the capacity to filter out a large amount of incoming sensory information, our conscious minds would be confused and overwhelmed, our perception fragmented, our senses overloaded and perhaps heightened as the mind focused even more intensely on what was coming in in a futile attempt to combat the confusion. Emotions, unprocessed, undefined and all muddied, may terrify us. People, as a major source of ever-changing sensory input may become a source of threatening overload we'd learn to seek to avoid.

We may adapt voluntarily and involuntarily, closing down conscious thought, using our senses one at a time in an unintegrated form or permanently shutting certain processing systems down.

We may preconsciously accumulate huge strings of unprocessed information for a later time when the sensory burden was reduced such as during sleep and whilst being unable to access this preconscious unknown knowing, may be in a triggerable state, like someone in a post-hypnotic state. Our chemistry would be different and our behaviour and our reactions which flowed from this would also be different from the 'usual'.

It would seem, therefore, that it is a natural phase in development that the system of interpretation should start up and take over from pure indiscriminate sensing. It would seem natural that curiosity would develop as the mind sought to further its interpretive repertoire in order to slot in better and dispose of incoming sensory information and, thereby, keep down the burden of what it experienced as incoming sensory chaos or bombardment.

I had the privilege of knowing a time before mind and I know the chaos of having mind start up too late to keep up with the flood of incoming information from a system of sensing which remained dominant and didn't become redundant.

I have known the adaptation of shutting down mind – sensory experience is no longer chaotic or bombarding once the mind no longer strives to file it or make sense of it. Yet, had I remained consistently in that state, using that particular adaptation, you would not be reading this book. I'd not have become functionally capable. Had we all been in that position and never climbed the developmental mountain of acquiring mind, then we would not have society as we know it and it is possible, maybe even probable, that in the absence of interpretation, we would rely on the sensory system of instinct and would far more resemble what we know as 'animals'.

One could reflect here on the evolution of 'humans' from the ape-like animals we once were. Some suggest that we evolved as a different species to those ape-like humans. Some figure aliens stepped in somewhere.

I figure that having opposable thumbs and being capable of creating an ever richer, ever more bombarding sensory environment, we progressively challenged our interpretive capacity to sort and file this progressively more complex information arising from our own expression and creation. As we did so, we developed mind and we progressively passed these acquired interpretive structures along to new generations in the form of what progressively evolved as ever more complex knowledge (including verbal, visual and physical language), morality and social convention.

In other words, what we know as 'normality' is a mutation that has taken many ages to refine and as we continue to express and create in progressively more complex ways, our minds will be further compelled towards finding ever more refined interpretive structures for this information – using megavitamins, amino acids, hyperbaric oxygen chambers or even computers to take some of the burden from us if necessary.

CHAPTER 9

'Seeing Ghosts'

I was about six when I first recall consciously confronting the choice of which system to rely upon. I can even remember the day.

I was walking down the street with my mother. I had a distinct sensing about which way to do something which was coming up. I could read the 'feel' of this, almost like it sat upon the air and this 'feel' instinctually told me that to do this thing in this way 'fitted'. Then I used my mind to judge whether this was the best things or not, the best way to do this thing. Using logic, it came to the conclusion that this sensed way was not the best way and that instead another way should be used. I felt convinced by this logic and, unable to see beyond it mentally, I went with the way it dictated. The result was that this way was not the best way after all and did not work out. At this I cursed myself for trusting in this new system – this system of interpretation, this 'logic' – and vowed I'd stick by 'my own system', that of sensing.

Everybody seemed to be on at me to use my judgement. Judgement would have been fine had I not had another system which often gave me the sensing that something was best done some other way from how mind or logic would assume was clearly either 'the only way' or 'the best way'.

I was about thirteen when I realised that other people didn't rely on sensing like I did. I knew about façades but having an intact system of sensing means that you can never fully convince yourself that these façades are real. You can lie, even to yourself for a time, but you can't lose or shake off the continual sensed lack of fit between the felt 'be' and the portrayed 'appear'.

When I was about thirteen, I had already bought into the socially learned game of façades but I'd bought into it late and clumsily, unable to fully integrate it. The data base for these façades were picked up mostly from TV characters and I understood mimicry and acting according to stored learned roles. But what had deeply distressed and depressed me around this age was when I tried to get others to stop playing what I saw as a game and to drop their façades. I'd assumed their own façades, like mine, were part of a non-integrated data base. I could clearly see straight past the surface and assumed they could too. The pattern of their real self in every form of expression contrasted sharply and with great clarity as an entirely different system to what they put on and the two stood out in clashing contrast as clearly as if they had been painted one black, one orange or had they been distinctly clashing notes. To relax and know it was safe to be my real self, I needed others to be willing and able to drop their bullshit too.

To my horror, when challenged to drop these façades, I found people defended them fiercely as though these were their 'real' selves. They took it further, considering my response to them weird and finally, when enough people had had similar responses, I eventually assumed they must have been right. I must have been somehow broken, deeply deluded, on the wrong planet. The thought that most people had cancer of the soul or had bought into a sort of social mass psychosis they called 'normality' was just a symptom of how crazy I'd actually become. On reflection, if I'd wondered where all the others like me were, they were probably heavily sedated somewhere either because they appeared incomprehensible or because they felt so crazy and depressed they felt safer that way.

It did finally get through to me that others wouldn't 'come clean' and be their real selves. I concluded that there must have been some socially agreed convention to pretend a lack of awareness. I couldn't quite understand why people would all agree to pretend like this, nor how they'd learned they were meant to or why I hadn't learned the same, but I figured that there must have been a good reason for it.

Perhaps it was dangerous to be one's real felt self, or at least always able to retrieve that self or drop all façades and admit its existence when it came to the crunch. Perhaps everyone but me had learned that. Maybe I'd been too thick or too preoccupied or too arrogant to learn it. Maybe I'd been too much 'in a world of my own' (which is where one is often assumed to be when in a consistent state of non-interpretation) and they'd all learned it because they didn't spend most of their time in the same way.

Perhaps the real felt self was somehow evil or shameful. It certainly often defied mentally-defined trendiness when expressed freely. It certainly was a far more potent and awesome force than the transient and shallow mock-expression that formed learned façades.

Perhaps, in some perverse way, the denial of real felt self was a way in which people felt safe with each other – where they knew where they stood.

On one level, one always knows where one stands with a real felt self. The inner self doesn't change, regardless of the outside cosmetics. It may become more of what it is but it is not defined by mind's judgements, comparisons or assessments of worth.

Yet, on another level, one always knows where one stands with a constructed non-real self. Rigidly sticking to some idea of what you are means you don't have the turmoil of flexibility of growth and change. It means you can let down your guard because you are your armour. It means no hurt can cut too deeply for it only cuts the surface and an overlaid one at that. It means control.

In spite of the fact it can be constantly adapted and reconstructed, the adaptations and reconstructions of false self occur *always* within the narrow structures of stored learning. As 'outrageous' and borderline, as individual and unique as any constructed non-self can be, at some level it will always be 'interpretable' according to stored learning, if only by translation from a similar or parallel image.

In a world which has learned to rely on the system of interpretation and either to deny or make redundant the system of sensing, it is unnaturally *natural* that people should have an unspoken consensus not to look beyond the surface and to believe and trust and live by the experience that what they see on the surface is all that there is. It is, perhaps, equally unnaturally natural that such people may be at once curious and threatened by challenging encounters with those for whom this is not their assumed reality.

It was my ex-husband who finally drew my attention to this. I had felt very sorry for all sorts of strangers who, it seemed to me, were making fools of themselves when it was 'so clear' that their behaviour had no connection to the real self in each one. It was a bit like the story of the Emperor's new clothes. I felt these people were very vulnerable because everyone would be able to see how distinctly they weren't able to be their true felt self. Sometimes I'd go so far as to reassure them, 'you can say that with your own voice' (meaning not using put-on intonation or a stored voice) or 'you can say that in your own words' (meaning using words and expression that came from their feelings and not learned phrases that fitted some image they'd learned to portray).

After many people treating me like some weirdo, my ex-husband argued with me that it wasn't *their* problem, it was mine. I was, of course, shocked and annoyed at this because I didn't have to bother acting on my empathy for them. I'd been bothered to reassure them *because I cared about them* (meaning their real felt selves which I could sense and clearly perceive through the cracks left by their façades). Eventually, he taught me that they were not pretending and really didn't know what I was on about. He explained that they really *did* experience these constructed mind-selves as their real selves and experienced put-on stored impressions of emotions as their real felt ones. Then I felt even more sorry for them and, after that, I felt sorry for me because I felt, sharply, my own alien-ness. They had the blessing of ignorance and, as my ex-husband put it, it was as though I was 'talking to ghosts'.

Visiting Self

Once it had really hit me that most people had lost the system of sensing, I eventually came to two interconnected questions; why did they lose it and why was this different for me?

When I was a child I felt what I later termed 'in the company of myself'. This didn't mean that I was on my own or spending time on my own. It meant that 'I', in this case referring to the 'I' that is mind, was spending time in the company of 'myself', referring to my 'real self' which is that self unaltered by mind where self-honesty is inescapable. That 'real self', I might call, 'the soul-self' to distinguish it from the constructed 'mind-self'.

Throughout childhood, I rarely experienced conscious thought. I'd been told many times, 'why don't you think?' Around the age of ten I'd watch the TV saying continually, 'what's happening', 'what's happening' and being told to 'just watch and find out'. I watched and I didn't find out because I couldn't interpret.

I couldn't just think because the state where I was most of the time was not a mind state at all, and so expecting me to think was like arriving in the remote mountains of Tibet and expecting to hear Swahili.

As I reached late childhood and approached early teenage, I did begin to have more conscious thought. It was repetitive, often very concrete, not very creative, but it was thought and with it came the evolution of a mind-self; some reflection of who I should be or what I should want or think or feel, what was valued by others and what was 'normal'. I developed a sharp contrast between what I'd always known as my self and this constructed self and I distinguished between the two, thinking only of the original, familiar one, as my 'real self'.

The more I found the world was pleased with my constructed mind-self and the less it rewarded (or actively discouraged) any display of my 'real self', the more I kept this mind-self for interaction and my 'real self' in private.

But it wasn't that simple. Here was a world which was showing me that everything I identified with was worth nothing and only my accumulative capacity, my data-base, my mind-self, was worth something. This angered me, it pained me, it alienated me and it confused me. It created external 'wars' and internal 'wars'. It put my real self into what felt like exile and it necessitated the need to 'visit my self'.

When I visited this self, I experienced being 'in the company of my self'. By contrast with all expression of the mind-self, these were enriching experiences in which I felt belonging and home coming. To visit myself, I sometimes just sat or lay or stood exactly where I was before being in the company of my self. So, what was the difference? What was the change? The difference was that I had disconnected from mind and as a result my relationship to my body changed too. No longer was my body taken account of by mind; it would become the shell which contained the real me and it would also become the tool through which I took in experience without mind. I'd returned to a state beyond conscious thought.

You might wonder what's the use of a self without mind, without thought, because many people think that thought *is* life and that without it there is no experience of life. Yet, without conscious thought, peripheral, preconscious experience, continues and so does sensory experience. It is sensed and accumulated but not interpreted at that time and yet there is still awareness. Information is still accumulated within preconsciousness where it may be later processed when consciousness returns and it becomes triggered voluntarily or involuntarily and is perceived consciously after it has been expressed – sort of listening in on oneself.

So what, perhaps, is the richness of the experience without mind or conscious thought?

Mind narrows experience. I remember sitting on the floor of a friend's house with a napkin and a nut. I explained that most people take the napkin and try to thread it through the nut as their way of expressing themselves. A lot gets lost. I explained that I spoke directly from the napkin but often it was hard to understand me, a bit like talking AppleMac in a Microsoft world – the formatting was incompatible.

Mind is necessary to communication involving interpretation but it is also the source of filtering out information according to stored learning of what is significant and what is not. Mind also dictates sensation, blocking it where it finds it inconvenient, overwhelming, uncomfortable or where it considers its own priorities more important and too important to be interrupted or muddied by sensation. With mind, one experiences sensation in an egocentric way and in terms of the personal significance of the sensation. What is missing is 'resonance'.

Without mind, sensation can be overwhelming. It may be perceived as highly inconvenient to the life mind has constructed. It may go against where mind expects to find sensation or what type or degree of sensation it expects to find in a given place or time or experience. Without mind, sensation can be a life shock and it can mess about with the structures of one's life created by mind. Yet, without mind, sensation can be as vast and as awesome as the sensory experience of the roaring of wild ocean waves crashing in the darkness of the night. It can be as deep and as high as the furthest depths and heights and as freely limitless and creative as the wind itself. It can be where one can feel a sensed resonance with things and creatures and people and the elements in a way mind can never experience no matter how much one strives with mind to reach for such experiences. It is here that one can touch magic and humility in a way with which the mind and its attempts at bigger and bolder and better and more outrageous, can never compete. And yet, to be abandoned to this state of pure self, this state of sensation, can be an imprisonment equal to that of a life dominated by mind-self and devoid of all capacity to visit, let alone functionally express, soul.

Now when I was about sixteen, I gave in to the pressure of a world which seemed only to want to see my mind-self and I stopped visiting my self. The result was acute anxiety, panic attacks and depression. I had the constant sense I'd lost something. I felt somehow 'disconnected' and found life to be flat and without hope; an endless play of scenarios I had no feeling for. After six months, I couldn't stand it any longer. Whether I was considered mad, weird, disturbed or not, I went back to visiting my self.

I began to stand in front of the mirror, staring into my eyes and looking for the real me looking back. At first, I couldn't see the real me at all, not in any gesture, not even in my eyes. I whispered my name to my reflection, trying to call me out but it was as though my real self no longer trusted the mind-self to which it had now conceded. My real self had been discarded, made redundant, ignored by the mind-self and it no longer trusted it. In just six months I'd succeeded in losing my soul just as others had.

I was lucky in that I didn't stay in that state. My mind-self eventually committed itself to constructing a life which would prove to my real self that it had a place in that life and was safe to return and that it was valued. It has taken years to really earn that inner trust and to find a calmness and humility of mind after it had tasted the addictive power of playing demi-god.

CHAPTER 10

War or Growth?

Conscious awareness is the start of reflection and choice. It is through reflection that we form a concept of self and identity and gradually acknowledge and come to terms with our separateness from all around us. It is here that we stop being a world unto ourselves and become an individual within the world. It is here we stop feeling immortal and begin to feel our own brittle mortality.

Because this transition takes place before conscious awareness has fully set in, it is generally not opposed in spite of the discomfort it can cause. Unopposed, what follows is growth. Sometimes, however, this stage of transition may bring initial growth but progress into war.

The age of about two to three is often a time of tantrums. It is also a time of great transition in which a child very sharply begins consciously to experience its own separate individuality and to assert itself as a separate self. Here communicative and purposeful language and social interaction, too, become increasingly more complex, reflecting the development of the conscious awareness and the system of interpretation.

Sometimes the world may be found to have too much impact, to be too directly confrontational. Watch the avoidance behaviours of some children around the age of three when approached or gazed at too directly or too personally before you have made his or her acquaintance and you may see a sort of 'exposure anxiety' or 'emotional hypersensitivity'.

Emotional hypersensitivity or exposure anxiety can be a natural stage for most children and the support of their environment together with their own repertoire of deflective and avoidance strategies probably protects them in getting through this and no long-term harm is done to their development.

Sometimes, a child going through this may not have the resources to cope. If the capacity to perceive or interpret is impaired, then even in a supportive environment, reassuring tones of voice, words, gestures or facial expressions may not be able to be consistently or cohesively interpreted with meaning. Expression may convey nothing, or worse, be sensed as clashing with the actual feeling of tension, annoyance or anxiety that is sensed as happening. Here the support that environment offers may be intangible, incomprehensible, imperceivable, confusing and even disturbing. The result may be that as conscious awareness dawns, such a child may be left too rawly exposed and, in effect, be unable to feel supported no matter how present that displayed support may be.

Similarly, sometimes it is not impairment in perceptual development of information processing that is at fault but that conscious awareness simply comes along too early. For some, this may leave the child 'too awake' before it has properly developed the concepts or strategies for seeking out the support needed to get through this time of transition and ways of avoiding and deflecting that which has too direct or personal an impact at this stage.

If this stage of transition comes along too late there may also be problems. Identity may have already become entangled with the system of sensing and the system of interpretation may be perceived as a challenge to identity and a threat with the potential to rob one of 'self'. Here the result may not be growth but war.

Life itself pushes us along certain developmental paths. Not only parents, but also siblings, family associates, neighbours, caretakers, teachers and society in general all *expect* development to take a certain course. Unless a child is convincingly labelled in a way that (correctly or incorrectly) presents it as unable to develop as expected, then there is likely to be direct or indirect pressure upon the child to develop as expected; 'normally' (and in some cases this happens even to children recognised as having a developmental disability).

When one is pressured at a stage at which one is not developmentally ready to go forward, there are three things that can happen.

If the pressure is constructively and informatively utilised in developing a programme for assisting development and this programme is realistically and achievably paced, then the stuck child may dare developmental steps that are always just that bit beyond him or her.

If the pressure is not realistically and achievably paced then overt or covert war may result.

Overt war is outright defiance in the form of attack, active avoidance or withdrawal. Covert war may take the form of compliance without identification with the behaviour one is being taught to perform. The war in this case may remain unseen but fester in the form of emotional or psychological defence that is sometimes (correctly or incorrectly) seen as distractibility, lack of interest, laziness or 'disturbance'.

Ultimately, however, most developmental blocks can be unblocked with the appropriate flexibility, open-mindedness, patience and approach.

For a range of reasons, I didn't make the transition from sensing to interpretation at the time most children do and I spent the first three decades of my life swinging between war and growth. Step by step, sometimes gradually, sometimes suddenly, a range of my own developmental blocks (biochemical, metabolic, perceptual, cognitive, emotional, psychological) were unblocked enough to free up development. With this came eventual trust of the system of interpretation and of mind and my own separateness as I distinguished between boundaries of self and other. That brought with it the beginnings of expression through social interaction and communication with others. Without properly making that transition, I may still be staring at a pink billiard ball, resonating with the colour in the absence of any concept of what I was staring at or its use, attempting to feel the bliss of 'becoming one' with it. Without properly making that transition, you wouldn't be reading this book I've now written and you would never know the system that was once in yourself which got left behind in a time before you identified yourself with it and probably before you can even remember.

Motivation

'Society' is a concept and experience based upon systems of interaction, communication and expression. All of these are born of having a shared, though culturally influenced, system of interpretation. Underlying these things is something much deeper; motivation and feelings, concepts and thoughts.

Starting at the deepest level, even before expression, is the driving force; motivation. For one can have motivation and yet not have moved beyond it to make the connections to action or expression. But without motivation, the best one can do is to rely on regurgitations of copied stored actions and expression which express nothing of self, thought, feeling or even sensation.

What drives motivation? Is it chemical, is it triggered by sensation or emotion or by thought?

If mind is born of the system of interpretation, and motivation is the product of thought, is motivation therefore missing in people who have not moved from sensing to interpretation?

If motivation is born of the synthesis of emotion and thought, what then if emotion is, as yet, undifferentiated from sensation?

If motivation is born of sensation, is this, alone, enough to drive action or expression?

If sensation is the stuff of chemistry, then can it be said that chemistry is the fuel behind the force of motivation?

Chemistry and Motivation

In a state of pure sensing, chemistry changes in response not to meaning within the environment but in response to changes in pattern and intensity. It also changes in response not just to energy but to particular patterns of energy found in all things.

I spoke earlier of edges. Edges are about the 'feel' carried by people, places, creatures, materials, objects. These are about variations in the flow and nature of energy.

Some energy is positively charged, some is negatively charged; both are shown to have effects on health and the general energy level of the in-dividual. In an air-conditioned office, under fluorescent lighting and sur-rounded by computers and other electrical appliances, there is generally a very positive charge in the air. It sounds great for you but it isn't. People with highly hypersensitive vision can actually sometimes see positively charged air particles which look something like minute silvery sparks in the surrounding air. Positively charged atmosphere can make people tired, agitated, restless, tense and lower their immunity, and these things show themselves in things like headaches, aches and pains and other minor common health problems. Many people use ionisers to change the balance of positive charge to negative charge which has the effect of reducing the health and energy sapping effects of a highly positively charged atmos-phere. When it rains or when one takes a bath, water and water particles in the air cause the atmosphere to become more negatively charged, so peo-ple feel more relaxed and refreshed. The balance and changes of positive or negative charges in the atmosphere cause chemical changes, affecting not just health but also mood and energy levels, all of which don't cause motivation but can certainly affect it.

Mood changes one's own energy field as can changes in the state of consciousness and proximity to another person (and I would say this can be physical or sometimes even spiritual 'proximity' or relatedness). This can have an effect on the energy field of others, whether a room, a creature, a material, object or person.

This shouldn't be so surprising. Grumbly people bring out nervousness and agitation in others. Animals can go 'prickly' at the presence of certain people. Some places have a 'feel' to them which makes the hair stand on end for no apparent reason. There have been occasional reports where there has been a marked increase in unexplained occurrences of appliances blowing up or going haywire or objects suddenly toppling without apparent cause when a particularly sensitive individual has been in an extremely distressed state. In all of these cases, I believe we are talking about the effect of certain types of energy when interacting with certain other types of energy. We are talking about edges.

Given three rooms all exactly the same and three people all looking and behaving similarly, I could enter each room and know from the way my own energy reacts as to whether their predominant edges at the time were fluffy, hard or sharp.

The same could be true of cats regardless of the colour of the cat or its behaviour. The same could be true of objects or materials that had picked up the energy of certain environments. The same could be true of three rooms, all looking the same but all having picked up the edges of the experiences that had happened in those rooms. In each case the energy of such a person, material, object, creature or place, would affect my chemistry, affecting the adjustment or resonance of my own energy. Yet, in this state I may purely respond like a measuring instrument and these changes may not cause the motivation to drive action or expression.

Sensation and Motivation

In sensing edges, these may bring out certain sensations in me, sensations resulting from changed chemistry, even of the sort to be called undifferentiated emotion-based sensations. At this point I may have involuntary reflex responses to these sensations but these are about brain, not mind and a reaction or reflex is not the same as action or expression which flows from motivation.

Some people say thought drives emotion and I'm sure it can. My experience is that emotion can also drive thought but that thought and emotion are separable systems which become integrated, even fixedly integrated with development as one progresses from sensing to interpretation. Yet emotion can drive physical response even without thought or awareness. The hand can involuntarily reach for or push away in emotional response to sensation. Expression, even interaction, at this point is not yet voluntary nor complex, not able to be accessed at will, with mind, yet these are its foundations.

Thought and Motivation

An experience may be stored without interpretation, purely on the level of impression. That impression may, on the most basic level, be a mapping of edges. On a more complex level, it may be a sensory mapping of an experience linked to a sensation. Still, there is no differentiation as to whether the experience is wanted or not and yet that stored connection may become triggered. That thought may, itself, drive the involuntary response of reaching for or pushing away or a replay of the physical responses that occurred with the original experience. This is the stuff of dreams. The basic difference between this and waking life is that the actions in waking life progressively become socially, purposefully and voluntarily directed.

Without interpretation, there is still experience. Without interpretation there is still sensation and emotion. Without interpretation there is a form of involuntary thought, expression and action. But the world without interpretation is a twilight zone between the consciously born and the consciously unborn, the semi-incarnate, perhaps karmically 'undecided'.

CHAPTER 11

Blah Blah and Ideas

Concepts begin to be born when the sensation or image of a sensory experience becomes stored and is later recalled as a prompt. It is stored first, not in mind, but on the level of impulse; a kind of 'body mapped' imprint.

Imagine that, without yet having developed interpretation as a consistent system, I came across what you'd know as 'a door'. I may sense its nature through my body without even touching it nor looking at it, and simply through 'resonance' may feel its lack of permeability and not attempt to walk through it. I may sense the shallowness of its depth and the release of this sense of density into open space on the other side. If I'd moved into physically-based sensing, I may test the nature of what happens to be a 'door' by tapping the panelling and the sonic feedback this gave me might confirm or deny what I already sense. Having had such an experience several times, this experience may then become linked to similar sensory experiences and further sensory exploration such as texture, smell or visual impression may further help categorise such 'door' experiences. Later, a similar sensing of a similar pattern regarding sensed permeability, sensed density or the sensed release of this density into open space on the other side may trigger not thought, but a recall of the body mapped impulse to test this sensing by tapping. On a more complex level, the sensing of 'the door' through smell may trigger the body mapped impulse of an earlier further exploration using texture, taste or visual mapping.

It is only later that one moves from nature to function of what is sensed. This is where one goes from 'door' as a sensory impression to the response of 'door' to action upon it. Such an action may be very confusing on a sensory level. On a sensory level, one can understand relative permeability or density but what is dense is not expected to move in response to impact and yet the door, sensed as dense, gives way under impact – a most curious and irreconcilable experience. I remember my own repetitive swinging of the loungeroom door for several years. I think it was something of a magic trick to me. It may make good sense when you are working within the system of interpretation where function is quite a concept but on the system of sensing, it is difficult to comprehend.

Other problems can also set up here once objects seem to take on their own action in response to contact. If the dense and non-permeable 'door' which gave way under impact had a large flat surface with sharp edges (corners) and was yellow and made of plastic that had a particular smell, taste and sound when tapped, then the similar plastic yellow table top may well become the testing ground for this 'magic trick' and you shouldn't be at all surprised when someone working without interpretation takes to repeatedly impacting upon it in such a way as to make it topple. If you have a 'door' of wood panelling that gave way in spite of the sensing that it was solid and could not be walked through, don't be surprised if the person starts walking into your wooden wall panelling, seemingly even more confused as to why some of these dense surfaces give way and others don't.

A similar example involves the dropping of objects through space. I found this an amazing experience and very freeing and took no account of what it was that I was dropping. What thrilled me also was to watch objects fall through space and be 'caught'. Toy cutlery went out the window into the roof guttering. Food bits went out the window into the roof guttering. Paper bits went out the window into the roof guttering. Later, I started letting my self go through space too and went about compulsively trying to comprehend this magical trick as I would let myself fall through space, straight onto the hard floor which would 'catch me'. I didn't cry or seem hurt as might have been expected. I giggled to myself because it was something equivalent to being on a special effects ride at Disneyland.

Something similar happened with food. I'd grasped the sensation of textures going into a hole in my face that is called 'eating' and whilst it seems such an unnatural thing to do without actually having sought the experience, I did learn the pattern of eating what was put in front of me. Without the discrimination that comes of interpretation, one gets the nature of the experience without the function. I went about playing with this 'trick', putting all sorts of things into that hole in my face – sand, dirt, paper, cardboard, rubber, plastic, shampoo, coins and all manner of plants (some poisonous). On a sensory level, I'd got the message quite clearly; putting things into the hole in your face is a source of sensory experience for textures, smells, tastes, the muscle feedback involved in chewing and swallowing the things and the excitement of being able to make wonderful sensory experiences (including things that were visually or auditorily a sensory 'buzz') part of me. Basically, I was a bit like that engulfing creature in the Pacman computer game. The effect on my body? I had all sorts of sensations happening but the concept of body, too, was without interpretation. It was just as much equipment in the game of these sensory experiences as was the sand or plastic or plants that went into it (as did food but generally with less choosing as food didn't always have such good effects sensorily).

These things can be difficult for society to accommodate, not just because it has interpretation concepts such as 'hurting oneself' or because it requires people to be 'functional' but also because it requires a large number of people to share things which means it needs people to relate to those things in relatively predictable and similar ways.

In the bathroom were things that were white, cold, smooth, with curved edges, all had metal fixtures (with quite contrastive sensory experiences) and which made the same sound when tapped and the same chinking sensation when bitten. They also all had running water. On a sensory level, nature comes first, pattern comes second and function comes last. On a sensory level all had a comparably similar sensory nature. On a pattern level, you could sit upon the edge of any of these and let water come out of your body and run downwards into the 'bellybutton' of these objects and all could be 'flushed' with running water as per the pattern. On a functional level, what the hell if these were thought of as basin, bath and toilet with specific assigned social purposes for each. Besides, the expectation to use the toilet made it a less safe realm in terms of exposure anxiety than using the sink or bath for which there was no such attention or expectation of self-expression.

The movement from nature to pattern to function is one that the world is quite impatient to have happen. Certainly, if this developmental shift is delayed beyond the age of three or sometimes five, people are in quite a panic. If, in spite of having grasped the patterns or even the function, one continually slips back to visit an earlier much more seemingly logical, sensible and familiar system, then one is thought disturbed, maybe crazy, maybe backward or sensorily impaired or the whole lot and one is either seen as an embarrassment to be shut away or as needing 'help'. One of the most noticeable absences of the developmental shift from nature to pattern to function is reflected not just in action and seemingly 'incomprehensible' emotional, cognitive or sensory response, but also in language.

Going back to the door before it is known in terms of function; before it is, in fact, 'door' (which is a function concept), it may have no word at all. Later, as one moves from non-physical sensing of what happens to be a door to physical-based sensing of what happens to be a door, its sound-concept is very unlikely to be 'door'. If you tapped the door, it may (depending on the door) tell you its name is 'took'. If it made a noise when it gave way under impact, it might say its name is 'rerr' if it drags on the carpet or 'ii-er' depending on the sound of the hinges. It may have no sound concept at all or the sound concept relating to the experience of door might come from the emotional experience of a sensory buzz associated with that door. So taking the example of the swinging door fascination, if this buzz experience brought out a little suppressed squeal (hard to write such a suppressed buzz squeal in letters), for me, the sound concept associated with the experience of door may well become this stored and later triggered sound. In someone in whom the buzz experience brought out an emotionally connected body expression movement such as the sudden staccato contraction of the fingers into outward-facing fists that jerk suddenly back towards the torso, this may become stored as something akin to a language sign associated with the buzz experience brought on by the swinging door.

So many things were 'degoitz'. 'Degoitz' was a sound pattern that became associated with an emotional sensation triggered by certain sensory-buzz experiences. For a long time, even though I'd learned the interpretation-based labels for certain objects, to me, these objects remained 'degoitz'. Instead of objects being labelled by their functional use, I'd labelled them by their shared sensory-emotional impact and these things, though functionally quite different, even perceptually quite different, were all the same on a sensory-emotional level. They were all 'degoitz'. At first 'degoitz' was used as a noun, later flexibly as an adjective-noun and later just as an adjective. 'So, describe this (clear deep red) glass will you please Donna.' 'Degoitz.' The natural assumption of someone who used only the system of interpretation would have been that either I wasn't listening, was being silly or was showing some kind of disturbed response. Later, 'degoitz' took on a grammatical form mimicking that used with other adjectives such as Elizabethan, Georgian, Edwardian and it became 'degoitzian'. (The origin of degoitz was degoitz-degoitz and probably came from associating the emotional sensation that went with tickling with the misheard words tickles-tickles.)

On the level of signing, there was an emotional experience that I called 'lemons'. In the language of interpretation this would be something like 'sensation of acute and intense exposure anxiety resulting in an involuntary and instinctual aversion response, akin to sensations underlying so-called shyness or agoraphobia'. This experience was called lemons because that was the word used for a related sensation. If you ate lemons (which I did), the taste caused the same sort of involuntary and instinctual aversion response. And yet the sensation of lemons was defined not by the object of a lemon, nor by its smell or its taste but by the physical reaction evoked by eating the thing with this name. This was also the same physical reaction evoked through being complimented or through conscious acknowledgement of having a great liking for another person or through the jolt to consciousness of sharply and rawly experiencing one's own expression before another person and sometimes even just before one's own consciousness.

Confused by my use of the word 'lemons', you'd have been more confused if you asked me to show you 'lemons'. Asked to show you 'lemons' (if the 'lemon' response itself did not preclude the ability to consciously dare and sustain the exposure of such personally confrontational expression) I'd have drawn my arms up at the elbows back in to the sides of my body with wrists flexed backwards near to the shoulders and palms facing outwards away from the body with fingers falling into the exposed cupped palms, together with the face somewhat screwed up with the top lip drawn up toward the nose and the eyes scrunched up as though squinting in extreme sunlight. The onlooker may have been quite confused by such a response and figured I'd not have understood and yet this very action demonstrates what 'lemons' can look like outwardly. Done instantly, this action could become the sign for 'lemons'. Later, 'lemons' became 'having lemons' and people still didn't understand. It got worse when they asked what sort of things caused lemons and I said 'fluffy people'. Asked to explain, I explained that fluffy edged people caused 'resonance' that gave me lemons. You can see why, as colourful as it may be, linguistically it would be an entirely different world if people could comprehend sensory-based language. Put into the language of interpretation (it took about twenty years to accumulate the means of concept translation) the statement 'fluffy edged people caused resonance that gave me lemons' becomes something like 'people who exude a free flow of emotional energy bring out similar patterns in me and through this I become so acutely and consciously aware of my own exposure before myself and others that this results in me having an involuntary and instinctual aversion response, akin to sensations underlying so-called shyness or agoraphobia'. Well, you tell me what five-year-old, ten-year-old, fifteen-year-old or even twenty-year-old is likely to struggle through that much translation mire in order to answer what seems a self-evident question and then answer how many people are likely even to conceive of the possibility that seemingly 'incomprehensible' language is actually capable of comprehensible, even illuminatory, translation into the language of interpretation that most people consider not just 'normal' but the only language.

Both on the level of verbal language, facial expression, body language and signing, the language of the system of sensing does not conform to the rules of the language of interpretation and it would be irrational to expect it to. Yet that is just what most people do expect. Even when it is accepted, it is considered aberrant, useless, pointless. Yet it often conveys experiences many people with interpretation have lost and could grow from knowing. Even understood, it is considered idiosyncratic. Yet, language and concepts within the system of sensing are repeated again and again by people devoid of interpretation or in whom interpretation is an inconsistent and secondary system who live on other sides of the earth and have never met each other. Not only do they generally find each other's concepts relatively comprehensible but many have come up with the same signs, words, actions and sounds for the same sensory and sensory-emotional experiences. I grew up in Australia and my concept 'lemons' when demonstrated within context to someone in the UK who shared the same sensation said, 'oh yes, disintegration feeling'. She had already, remarkably, come across someone else who she'd never previously met but who spontaneously 'used her word' for the same feeling.

CHAPTER 12

Progress?

From the Sensory to the Literal

As one moves from non-physical-based sensing to physical based sensing, the earlier stage can still remain. Identity is one of the reasons why one lets go of an earlier stage. Another is the capacity to trust and become familiar with the next stage. That can depend a lot on how consistent and predictable sensory-perception and information processing are and how rewarding and comprehensible the new experiences are by contrast to those within an earlier stage. Sometimes, one can rigidly hold on to an early stage and be blocked from taking the next step. If this happens in early infancy before the birth of interpretation and 'mind' then such a block cannot really be called a 'decision'. Even in the event that the mind is willing to go forward, the will, or the soul, may be unable to trust not just the environment but the mind itself, particularly if the sensory-perception from which interpretation springs is inconsistent, fragmented or for some reason found unreliable.

If this happens at such an early stage, psychotherapy can do little to help, for the mind itself may be intact and committed to moving forward. Working with the will and getting the will to trust the mind is something altogether different and much harder to tackle. The mind is reasoned with consciously. The path to the will, however, is an indirectly confrontational one. The home of will exists in a place before the dawning of consciousness and it is only there that it is to be met and gradually helped to edge its way progressively towards trust and daring to connect with consciousness.

If the path from sensing to interpretation goes smoothly, the first steps are in moving from sensory mapping to the mapping of pattern to ascertaining the nature of something or someone by pattern. From there, one can come to map not only nature but function and purpose or even a range of functions or purposes.

At first the idea of interaction is not there, for within the system of sensing it is not self plus other, nor even self or other. Within the system of sensing, familiarity is a matter of empathy and empathy is a matter of resonance and mergence. By contrast, the system of interpretation requires the maintenance of separateness and the mechanism of 'reflection' which springs from these encounters.

To move from resonance and mergence to separateness and reflection would seem an unnatural direction, for within the system of sensing, one is drawn into experiences in which one gains nothing without the loss of the boundaries which constitute all sense of self and other. Even as mind steps in, one may be unable to retain separateness within mind, merging with one's own mentally evoked sensations and returning, perhaps, to consciousness without the capacity for reflection.

To move to separateness, one must seek not to sense but to know. To sense involves mergence. To know involves retaining separateness.

Gradually, the diving feeling of mergence may feel more like being dragged into the depths beyond control. The freedom of mergence may gradually come to feel like suffocation. Perhaps rarer and maybe even worse, the transition is half done and one swings between one and the other with the ensuing effects on identity formation. One part may go forward with mind and separate sense of self as a personal entity. The other may avoid mind, unable to identify with it or even find it safe or rewarding, and may relate to self not as a personal entity but as a tool for mergence and resonance within the system of sensing. Such would be a state of two co-existing states of mind; one a waking dream self and the other the conscious mind aware of its existence, perhaps capable of suppressing it, but unlikely to be able to control it.

The mind may go forward to develop literal interpretation but without the sensual self intact, it may not be able to conceive of a level of interpretation beyond the literal; more complex interpretation which takes account of personal significance. This is the birth place not of mind, but of false self.

From Sensing to Personal Significance

The level of the literal is enough to be able to use much of the language of interpretation on all levels; the language of touch, visual language and auditory language. But literal interpretation relies upon logic. Sensing is about what is. Logic is about what appears.

Trouble starts when the sensing of what is seems totally incongruent with what appears. Which system does one choose to go by? Sensing, unlike logic, can't be 'tested'. One must simply trust and find out. Social learning pays lip service to trust but teaches us not to trust anything we can't test out. It teaches us that sensing is a secondary system. Perhaps it is no mistake that those seen as 'simple' are more likely to rely upon sensing or believe in it. Perhaps 'simple', rather than referring to 'intelligence' refers to how adept one is at using the system of interpretation. In part, that too does not depend so much on intelligence as, perhaps, the relationship between one's systems and one's identity and the way social learning has or has not crushed adherence to and trust in one's first system; that of sensing.

Yet even those who progress from the sensing to literal interpretation are sometimes mistakenly considered 'stupid'. Others may realise being literal does not reflect upon intelligence and see these people as 'naïve'. Though they use mind, what is missing is processing beyond the literal to the level of personal significance. One person sees a table another sees who's table it is and why it's probably there. We are taught to strive for the latter and yet with all its advantages, the significant is also the home of false self and all its games within the realm of appear.

The person without interpretation may be adept at relying on body and soul within a well developed system of sensing and experience themselves as 'alien' to those who live within the mind realm of literal interpretation.

The sensing person may not bother with the meaning, purpose or function of people, creatures, places or things (even body) within the environment just as the literal person may not bother, nor even conceive, of the hierarchy, game playing and image making of the person who lives in the world of personal and relative significance. We, on this earth, look for aliens, yet they stand among us. We come across them every day. And when we do, we have mistranslations, misunderstandings, misinterpretations and misjudgements. Those in the world of false self may see through the glasses of hierarchy. Those in the world of mind may see through the glasses of labels and analysis. Those in the world of soul may be unable to see at all that which you define yourself by and yet sense you as you truly are. And all are right and all are wrong according to their own system and that of the others they come into contact with.

In the realm of sensing, sense of self and sense of other are irrelevant.

In the literal world of logic there is self and there is other but one shifts between the complete sense of one or the other but fails consistently to experience the two simultaneously within the context of one another (in spite of being able to grasp the concept theoretically). Here one knows not just sensation but requirement: need. Here one knows capability: can. Here one may learn expectation: should. Here, one's mental concept of self is as honest as the senses and perception allow.

The progression from the literal world of fact collecting logic to that of personal and relative significance is one from self *or* other to simultaneous self *and* other.

Logic is the birthplace of the accumulative mind, even the curious mind, but when one moves to personal and relative significance, one moves to discrimination and choice. Here one knows not just sensation, impulse, compulsion or need, but like and wish.

Here one dreams and imagines, altering the image and then seeking the image in reality. Strangely, the progression from sensing to personal significance is not one of moving outwards into life, but moving inwards into mind, yet a particular part or framework of mind; the mental representation of one's dreamed up conception of self in relation to all experiences. The mind concept of self (and other) now is likely to not just be a representation of what is but of what one wishes or fears oneself (or others) to be. Misunderstanding may be born of a literal mind but madness is the stuff of false self. Development may have its costs as balance becomes an increasingly precarious task.

CHAPTER 13

Beyond an Exchange of Cultures

The difference between sensing and interpretation would seem broadly to encompass what gets called a 'culture'; a shared way of relating, communicating and ideas or concepts, a way of identifying oneself. But this difference makes for more than 'cultural' exchange too, for cultural exchange relies only on swapping tools of interpretation within the same system.

Cultural exchange involves the sharing or swapping of different forms of the language and ways of interpretation all of which have arisen from essentially the same sensory, perceptual and cognitive mechanisms. Yet, hard as one might try, it may be much easier for a human being with interpretation to have a cultural exchange with an octopus with interpretation than it may be for a person with interpretation to comprehend someone who functions without it, primarily on the level of sensing.

Human beings have created (interpretation-based) fantasies about aliens, always somehow expecting or assuming a system of interpretation at some level. This must make interpretive human beings feel quite smug and in control for they'd be able to find a level of translation with which to interact and communicate with such beings. But what if such beings were not advanced at using the system of interpretation but yet infinitely superior to any known interpretive human being at using the system of sensing?

At every level, the sensing creature is different from the interpretive one.

The interpretive creature, particularly humans, have come to rely predominantly and primarily on vision or hearing. The sensing creature, human or otherwise, may use senses more flexibly, relying on non-physical sensing, body-mapping, touch, sonics and smell. With interpretation being less important than sensation itself, vision and hearing probably don't become the primary senses they otherwise would.

Even when the visual and auditory are used, they may be used by the sensory being in a preconscious and peripheral way rather than directly and consciously as with the interpretive being.

Storage and recall, too may be different. The sensory being may use serial memory, storing long strings as a single chunk. Recall of the information may be triggered rather than accessed. They may store experiences or form concepts using categorisation and relationship based more on the sensory nature of these things than on their 'meaning'.

The interpretive being, relying on the conscious mind, may be more limited in the ability to store even if accessing to information may be more voluntarily accessible. The storage of information for the interpretive being may be more likely to be related to the meaning of an experience, with its logical or literal interpretation or its categorisation being somehow related to its relative or personal significance.

Reliance upon different forms of consciousness also has implications for the concept of 'social'. The person functioning on preconscious autopilot is governed by the will. The person functioning on a conscious level is governed by the mind.

The preconscious mind responds to an indirectly confrontational approach and finds a directly confrontational approach jolting, even an imposition. Most of the social world as people know it is not indirectly confrontational and is becoming even less so.

The conscious mind responds to a directly confrontational approach and experiences this as interaction. Competition, comparison, hierarchy and strategy make sense within a directly confrontational approach.

Relationship to one's own expression, too, may be extremely different for the two groups. The freed expression of someone in a state of preconscious autopilot, regardless of how revolting or spectacularly impressive, may be experienced as having no connection at all to 'I'. After all, 'I' is a concept of mind, not of will. Will is the 'it', well before the time of 'I'.

When the 'it' expresses something, there is no sense of choice. Choice, too, is not just a concept but an experience of mind. 'I' may have the power to discriminate, to choose, even if the only exercise of that choice is in the stifling of 'it', but 'it' has no concept of restraint (although instinct to withdraw or avoid/divert expression because exposure is felt too intensely may seem like 'restraint').

Consider this in the context of interpretive assumptions of the relationship of oneself to one's expression. Consider this in the context of self-reflective concepts such as 'choice', 'pride', 'enjoyment', 'achievement', 'courage', 'application' or even the relevance of sharing, so fundamental to social interaction as most interpretive beings know it (and assume to be 'natural').

The concept of body, too, is part of this. In a preconscious state, body may be experienced neither as part of self nor part of 'I'. Expression through body in gear on preconscious autopilot, may mean that if the 'I' of mind even coexists at this stage, body may well be experienced as a separate entity from 'I'; a tool used by 'it'. Consider this in the context of social touching where interpretive people seek to share 'I' with one another through physical contact. Consider this in the context of personal and emotional response to the physical pain, cold or discomfort of the body and all the social behaviours and expression considered 'normal' associated with such sensations. Sure, the sensations may be felt, but uninterpreted and, moreover, devoid of personal interpretation, even the concept that one should care what happens to 'body' may be an extremely foreign concept.

Within the system of interpretation, concepts such as time and space are taken for granted. Yet these may be distinctly different for those who live primarily by the system of sensing. Time may be thought to be experienced by the body but it is my view that part of the way the body interprets time is governed by the experience of the mind. Linear time is a perceptual experience, just like colour.

There are those creatures, human and otherwise, who experience colour in very different ways to how 'most people' do. I used to see the most exciting and beautiful pastel coloured rainbows in a piece of ice. I could see so-called 'flesh' tones as they are represented in Impressionist paintings full of blues and greens, purples and yellows.

Time, too, like the concept of left and right seemed constructs which remained flexible for me. When I drew things 'in mirror' image, I hadn't realised my mind had reversed what was seen. Or, perhaps, it had not. For I had merely drawn what was seen at that time. So, too, have I had not just the experience of future 'memory' but also of space completely reversing and having come out of a building I'd entered a few minutes before found the entire street and everything in it completely reversed. I had a hard time getting home (even once I'd located my car). I had to drive the entire route away from my home before being able to orient myself in driving back in the, seemingly irrational choice, of the opposite direction to where instinct told me my home was.

That time is linear and direction within space is fixed, are taken by interpretive beings to be indisputable facts. Yet it may well be, that just as a dog does not perceive colour as humans do, so too may linear time and fixed direction within space be little more than perceptual constructs born of a certain way of processing information. Imagination, too, is a tricky topic. Imagine for a moment what it is to imagine. It involves being able consciously to put together a synthesis of fragments in a coherent way so as to form a running mental scenario.

In the sensory realm, before interpretation becomes the primary language of experience, vision is not the predominant sense. Until the will has come to know the restraint imposed upon it by an interpretive mind, the meta-representation of experience is not highly developed nor yet terribly relevant. Without interpretation, each stored sensory fragment may remain separate. This synthesising of information is the job of meaning; the discriminatory relevance and recognition of purpose, function or relatedness. Those who live without interpretation may be wildly creative, often more freely so than someone governed and blinkered by the dictates of an interpretive mind which controls what it expects to be expressed and how.

Ways of relating within society are formed predominantly by the actions and words of people for whom interpretation is their primary system. These people generally find concepts such as gender, race, age, sexuality and functional ability to be important. Such people easily identify themselves and others by these things as primary forms of identification. These identifications then form the basis of certain ways of thinking and relating.

Look at your hand. Focus on your hand. Smell it, taste it, touch it, look at it and put your ear close to it. Do you experience the microbes upon it? If you didn't know, in theory, that they were there, would they exist? Existence is about experience and it is about what is foreground and what is background and just how foreground or background something is. If it is background enough that one cannot perceive it, it does not exist in experience and one, therefore, would not conceive of it unless taught, regardless, to take theoretical account of what can't be experienced. Now, imagine that you were looking through a very powerful microscope at your hand. Imagine you were using the most powerful technology which could detect infinitesimal odours and sounds or detect taste millions of times more acutely than the human can. For that moment, these microbes may exist on an equally foreground level as one's own hand, not just theoretically but through experience. So too may interpretive concepts such as gender, race, age, sexuality and functional ability be such background information as to be not only unimportant to a sensory being but sometimes even imperceivable non-concepts.

Dishonesty is not just about lying, it is about the mind's denial of the will. If I convince myself I feel something, even conjure up the pseudo emotion and follow it through in a logical assumption of action or expression, then I am dishonest. If I listen to mind about my surroundings, judging them to be safe when my soul (if not already stifled to the point of being so background as to no longer be experienced) on a feeling level attempts to tell my mind otherwise, this is dishonesty.

Society appears to promote honesty but most of its structures rely on dishonesty. Dishonesty is not just from others but from oneself. It is born of false self and requires some grasp of and adherence to the system of interpretation. It is about the world of 'appear' and about game playing in which one presents the 'appear' under the guise that it is the 'be'. Remarkably, it commonly fools those who live primarily by interpretation, particularly if the dishonest person is being dishonest even with themselves. Having lost sensing, most people use the 'appear' as foreground information. To the sensory being, the 'be' is the foreground regardless of the degree to which one is socially trained and pressured to respond to the 'appear' as though, falsely, it was the 'be'. I used to go around unable to perceive the 'appear' because it was so background that only the 'be' stood out. The 'appear' would strike out like an unannounced phantom from nowhere. Later, I became 'bilingual' in acquiring and becoming reasonably able to use the system of interpretation as well as the system of sensing. For a long time, it confused me greatly that others would 'pretend' they didn't know that the 'appear' they were presenting wasn't the 'be'. Even when I gave in to the belief that the 'appear' was what one was meant to go by (and one was meant to pretend this was the 'be' and join in some societal conspiracy not to admit one knew otherwise), I still couldn't fight off foreground awareness of the 'be', not only in how I experienced others but also myself. It is a difficult life when someone stands before you expressing the emotions their mind expects them to have about something when the 'be' (what's between the lines) shouts out the opposite feeling to what is expected or being portrayed. All the more shocking, when, in empathy for the soul being sold out, one makes the sell out clear only to be laughed at, shouted down or ignored!

The concept of who one is is also different in the interpretive world of 'appear'. In the world of 'appear' one comes to identify with and defend, even brutally and with great conviction, the idea that one is one's appear. The sensory being who has acquired the system of interpretation as a second language, may buy into the appear. Yet, unlike the interpretive, he or she may be unable to become convinced that this is self.

Going even further, the self of the mind is not the same as the self of the soul. In fact, they may be utterly at odds with each other. Often, the mind

suppresses the will and the will occasionally and sometimes embarrass-
ingly breaks through and seizes control as soon as the grip of the mind is
weakened. Whilst the self of the mind may be corrupt and even a false self,
the self of the soul, although perhaps not fitting with the mind's socially
learned conception of righteousness, is not tainted by false self. So, not
only may the 'I' be a construct and not truly know its deeper, truer self, but
nor may any interpretive being know anybody else. Without the capacity
to sense, beyond mind, beyond interpretation and beyond the appear, all
else is transient construction, nothing substantial nor lasting. It is little
wonder that sensory beings often know no loneliness until they step into
the system of interpretation. It is perhaps equally little wonder that the
greatest emotional plague faced by those who live primarily by interpretation is a loneliness that can't be shaken off. This empty aloneness is also
possibly one of the greatest driving forces of the many social diversions
which constitute a sort of epidemic of spiritual cancer, a socially promoted
epidemic that leaves people susceptible to everything from smoking to
violence, co-dependency and exploitation.

Even the concept of 'God' itself is different for those who live primarily
by the system of interpretation. People living by interpretation don't sense
or feel 'God', but generally think about, even test, 'God' with mind. In this
way, 'God' is generally conceived of as being something outside of themselves, something much greater, unfathomable with mind, something that
is constant and not transitory. They may conceive of 'God' as far more all
knowing than they with their petty human conscious thinking. Yet this
may not be a reflection on how little humans are, so much as how little
they make themselves when they reduce themselves to mind. People who
rely primarily on interpretation may think of 'God' as knowing the bigger
picture, as having some instinct for their place in the scheme of things
which the mind in its sometimes arrogant recklessness cannot fathom.
They may think of 'God' as beyond false self and somehow infinitely capable of empathy, yet it may be their very denial and non-use of their own
capacity to sense which has made all but shallow interpretive empathy a
redundant system. They conceive of 'God' as somehow pure and yet this is
probably the projected purity they themselves lost sight of, left behind. It
is, perhaps, no coincidence, that their concept of 'God' bears such a similarity to their own sensory being, left behind for most, too long ago to remember. These people may actually be reaching, not outside of themselves
as they believe, but for their own souls from which they've become
estranged.

It is, perhaps, no mistake that those who reach for faith with mind, do not find it even if they can refine the rituals. The soul may well have long since given up trust in the mind and wouldn't answer its knock upon soul's door when it reeks still of the taint of fear-driven insecurity, mistrust and acquired arrogance. Yet, there are those who lose faith in mind and all of its constructs and structures, who 'suddenly' find they have 'found God'. Though the mind even at such a point may dictate and contort the experience at the hands of inescapable socially learned constructs, could it not have been that what was found in such a state was not some external 'God', but one's own soul?

To the sensory being, the nearest concept to 'God' may be one's own soul. Resonance is the empathic mechanism through which the sensory being feels the soul (or 'God' in all things). If what the sensory being feels is energy, then it is energy that is encapsulated within various bodies but also energy which exudes beyond it into the feel of a room. It is carried in the wind and an ocean tide. It is carried in the earth and in every rock.

Those who believe in 'God' have said that God is all pervasive; everywhere and in everything. Those who live primarily by the system of interpretation may have much to consider regarding their ideas about fear of death and the preservation of life, if they dare. It is, perhaps, no mystery, that sensory beings, who have not bought into the system of interpretation, have no fear of death nor even physical danger.

I had wanted to fly for so long, as long as I could remember. Even in my early teens, I wanted to jump from the top of a building in order to fly. My theory was simple. I couldn't fly because my body wouldn't leave me. If I could make it leave me, make it detach, I could fly and be free in a way I felt I never could be in life. I did not feel I was being suicidal because I didn't identify with my body. I wasn't thinking of killing myself. I wasn't thinking of an end to experience. I left my body in sleep and for periods throughout the day so I simply wanted to retain that state, not be dragged back to body. At various times when friends experienced me in this state I was thought of as disturbed, suicidal. Yet I was always happy in this state, as happy as anyone standing at the gates to potential heaven might be. I knew about death and suicide. That was about tragedy and sadness and killing one's self. Death was about an end to experience. This was not about suicide and death. I knew my self would be freed, not ended.

Over the years, I thought a lot about suicide and what it means. In a depressed state, wanting my body to detach permanently was wanting an end to all experience. Certainly, there have also been times when I have felt I've been dying inside a living body, my soul ebbing away. Leaving this world in a negative state is a sad and tragic thing. So is living in this world in a healthy body with little or no soul left in it.

CHAPTER 14

Multiplicity

'Languages'

In Webster's dictionary, language is defined as a system of words prevalent in one or more countries or communities or in a profession. It is also listed as a system of symbols or rules for computer programs. Words themselves are defined as any sound or combination of sounds forming a meaningful element of speech, conveying an idea or alternative ideas and capable of serving as a member of, or substitute for, a sentence.

Within the system of interpretation, language is systematised and passed down rather than evolving directly from the sensory or emotional experiences they spring from. Interpretive language requires much more translation from the symbol to the experience-concept a word refers to, whether in spoken language or in sign. There are two signs for toilet, for example, within the sign language known as Makaton. One involves forming a 'T' shape with the hands with one held vertical and the other laid horizontal over the top of it. In sensory-based language, this would far better convey 'table' than it would toilet. The other sign for toilet involves the pointer and middle fingers together, placed over the heart area and drawn vertically down the torso. In sensory-based language this would relate the sonics made by running these fingers over the texture of one's shirt, the texture of the fabric or skin in that area or that that part of the body had an itch. The sensory-based mime-sign for toilet which I've used is that of miming the pulling down of trousers. The 'T' sign triggers no instant connection to any physical or sensory-based experience relating to toilet, nor does the two fingers on the chest. The mime-sign, however, does. Even the deaf-sign for milk, involves something of a mime-sign reminiscent of milking a cow. Whilst a little closer to a sensory-based relating to milk, most people have never hand milked a cow nor even see it done. The mime-sign for milk, by contrast, involves the mimed tipping up of a glass to one's mouth. Of course, this is basically the sign for drink rather than being specific to milk, but the advantage is that, requiring little translation from symbol to sensory-experience it is much more quickly accessed, especially for those who have some difficulty accessing their own symbols. Clarification of exactly what drink can always happen once the request for a drink is at least made.

In terms of spoken language, the verbal sentence 'where is the cat?' requires much translation. To anyone aware of the sensory sound experience made by the object in question – the cat – simply making the sound 'brroook' when no cat is about says the same thing but, by contrast, requires virtually no translation time and far less information processing time and space.

'Can I have some paper please' could be made much more economical. Among those who've been free enough to explore the sensory nature of things, 'cr-cr-cr' (with a guttural 'c') in the absence of any useable paper about when said between those who are well acquainted with the sound paper makes when crumpled could, with use, be even easy to understand, especially when combined with the mime-signing of paper crumpling.

'The surface of this paper is really bright', could be stated merely by tapping the surface of the paper and then mime-signing 'bright' by bringing the fists up to the eyes and releasing them suddenly into flexed outspread palms, dispersing out to the sides like falling fireworks – indicating the explosiveness of brightness and the sort of sunburst effect one has when looking into light. The statement 'this paper is very bright' is translated into the same signing with the extension of the mime-sign for big – that of outstretched arms with palms brought in to face each other (containing the space of 'bigness'). Verbally, it would read, 'paper, bright-big'. 'I don't want the bright paper' could be expressed quite simply by pushing the paper away or even mime-signing such if the paper in question was not present. If asked why it's not wanted and the paper wasn't present, it might translate 'cr-cr-cr + sign for bright+big'.

Language complexity is not always a reflection of intelligence. Sometimes it makes far more sense to use the simple form and reserve one's resources for other things. It takes humility, intuition and pragmatism to see that both the language of interpretation and the sensory-based language of the soul could have their time and place as complementary systems.

'Culture'

The word 'culture' is defined by Webster's Dictionary as, 'the customs and civilisation of a particular time or people'.

A culture is born of a shared sensory-perceptual experience and the sensory-perceptual world of the primarily interpretive being is a very different world from that of the sensory being.

One person may see a fence forming the boundary of a property in order to keep creatures out or in. Another may see coarse, brown, spiky, vertically running fibres of a particular sound which give way somewhat when bitten. When in close proximity to one another, one may see these adhere to form a relatively impermeable surface of some span which stands in a vertical and horizontal, relatively flat-surfaced form running through space but pulled to, or springing from, a flat surface of an entirely different form running beneath it in a vast expanse (the ground).

A culture can be about one's social system. This is not purely who one is social with, but one's system of being social.

The social world of the interpretive being may involve utilising a learned interaction system involving what is known as (interpretive) 'language' and (interpretive) 'manners'.

The social world of the sensory being may involve using a learned interaction system involving what is known as (sensory-based) 'language' whether physically-based or non-physically based. The sensory being may use sensory-based (non-mental) empathy through resonance in a relationship between sender and receiver in which the receiver loses their own separateness in merging with the sender as part of the mechanism of acquaintance before returning to the unmerged state of its own entity.

Those who live primarily by the system of interpretation live, effectively, in the same physical world as those who are primarily sensory beings (in the sense of the earth or universe). However, they move in different sensory-perceptual and social worlds or 'cultures'. Just as each can be 'bilingual' in terms of 'language', each could be 'multicultural', able to move between culture-worlds as needed and able to interpret for those more proficient in one system than the other.

The sensory-based social system could be important for crossing boundaries to know the nature of something which cannot be fathomed with mind or through language. The interpretive-based social system could be important when subjectivity is required (which requires an intact sense of self).

Sensory-based perception could be used where interpretation limits the understanding of the true nature of what is being experienced or its aesthetics. Interpretation-based perception, on the other hand, could be used most widely where purpose (rather than nature) needs to be taken account of.

Imagine a world where all had the flexibility of both systems, where the social cancer born of false-self was not as pervasive nor promoted as natural, where true empathy born of resonance took at least equal place with learned 'manners' and the performance of socially expected empathy behaviour. In such a world, one would retain the ability to lose separateness and feel not just for someone or something but *as* someone or something.

'Identity'

Identity is about how we recognize ourselves in relation to others. Those who are monolingual and monocultural, either in the system of sensing or the system of interpretation, will have a very different sense of identity.

The system of interpretation involves retaining one's separateness from others whilst having a simultaneous sense of self and other. It is this simultaneous sense of self and other which is necessary to being able to compare or contrast ourselves with others, whether objects, creatures or human-creatures. To those who live primarily by the system of interpretation, identity is an important concept but also leads to a feeling of alienation from others.

In the absence of a clearly defined identity, it has become almost 'natural' to latch on to one or a series of constructed identities. Yet, even with these, consciously or unconsciously, one feels alienated from others even if they also go primarily by the system of interpretation.

The capacity to compare and contrast also makes those who live primarily by the system of interpretation competitive. It is the development of this which may be responsible for people being more likely to buy into symbols of transient and pseudo 'respect' and 'achievement'.

The person who lives primarily by the system of interpretation, having such capacity for self definition, is also more prone to limit him or herself to certain experiences over others. Unable to relate on an equal level to all creatures and objects and far more subject to loneliness and insecurity as their transient structures are challenged to change with time, the only security may be in sustaining the same crowd, the same scene and calling this 'choice'.

The primarily sensory being exists in a world of all self with no simultaneous sense of other, or all sense of other with no simultaneous sense of self. Because of this, the sensory being may never know the concept of loneliness even though they may sense it in resonance with someone or something feeling loneliness. Competition, too, may not exist, nor the winning and losing it entails.

The sensory being may be more drawn to resonate with certain entities over others and may know loss and disruption. Yet, it may adapt better in terms of attachment for it knows company through resonance. Because of this it may be able to replace resonance felt with a lost human being with the resonance felt with a cat or even an object without this carrying the sort of reflective hierarchy this might carry for someone who goes by the system of interpretation.

Sensory beings may be relatively indiscriminate, latching on not to the identity of others, but to the warmth or energy of their entity. Depending on the environment and availability of alternatives, resonance, too, can be a compulsive and addictive orientation and one which, when indulged in to extremes, can leave one functionally disabled.

Someone living by the system of interpretation can consciously or unconsciously feel empty and fragile when relying on pseudo identity. Similarly, the sensory being can find the return to the separateness of self entity so cold and vulnerable by contrast with the warmth and completeness found in resonance with a sense of other that return to self can become progressively less attractive, less tolerable and less possible to sustain. The result may be a sort of refusal to live through one's own body as a separate entity; an energy-level, soul-level refusal to in-carnate. Long term, this would make someone functionally disabled. Their development of communication and social skills would be seriously stunted even though there may be no sign of mental or physical disability, although ultimately, with lack of use, mind and body would also, eventually be underused, undersized, underdeveloped. Even in those who did live at least part time through their bodies, an undeveloped ability to compare and contrast reflectively would make sensory beings vulnerable in situations requiring judgement and personal choice based upon good judgement.

Those who have acquired a multi-identity, able to move between the system of sensing and the system of interpretation, may strike the best balance. Such people would be able to be functionally able, secure in his or her independence yet able to seek assistance, capable of seeking social company as a separate being yet equally capable of deep true empathy, less prone to insecurity, loneliness and addictive behaviours and yet capable of both feeling and responding to these things in others.

CHAPTER 15

Psychic?

The term 'psychic' is one that provokes a lot of different reactions; awe, disbelief, fear. There are those who confuse the mind-based capacity to analyse or 'psyche someone out' with being psychic. There are those who confuse wishful thinking and imagination with intuition. Anyone can use the word 'sense' when what they really mean is 'think', 'believe', 'imagine' or 'wish'. But all of these things are of the mind. Sensing, however, is not.

When someone truly senses something, it also has nothing to do with false self. It involves no necessary connection with the personal significance or relative significance. It involves none of the discrimination of mind in terms of hierarchy. The mundane is equally as likely to be sensed as the catastrophic.

When someone can truly sense without mind or false self, it could frighten some people and have others see it somehow in the context of the divine. This is because most people have 'knowing' which comes from mind. Their means of finding out something is generally always explainable in terms of the direct experience of the physical senses. They can say 'I knew that because I saw you X, Y or Z', 'I knew that because I read about someone else who did X, Y or Z', 'I knew that because I could hear how…'. When people have the 'knowing' born of sensing, it can't be traced to an experience of mind via the physical senses. It is more a matter of energy.

One can respond to the body-mapped pattern of energy sensed and that response may demonstrate a 'knowing' that is seen as 'psychic'. So, for example, I seemed constantly to surprise people who were closely involved with me when I would phone them up out of the blue – very often this would coincide with their just having mentioned me or been writing to me or thinking of me. By contrast with their other friends or acquaintances, the number of such occurrences was very high, leading people to believe there was some kind of psychic occurrence happening. Someone summed this up saying, 'you don't have to call Donna, you just have to think loudly about her.' I would have said it was not about thinking loudly but feeling strongly. In those days my 'doors' were open, too open, and too often. I've fortunately learned how to shut those doors and to use them at least more by choice than purely by resonance.

Responding in a way indicative of psychic intuition gives no explanation of how the 'knowing' happened. Such explanations involve the mechanics of reading a preconscious mechanism using conscious awareness, a bit like listening in on one's own dream.

I have experienced such dreaming, my unconscious mind having a dream with my conscious mind simultaneously present and butting in with the mental reminders of some external observer. My non-sleeping mind would remind my unconscious dreaming self that 'I' don't really live there, 'I'm' not really that age, this isn't really happening.

Always when such things happen, these reminders are not experienced within the thought of my own character in the dream, but external to the dream. These experiences are perhaps part of why I have been able to use my conscious mind to explain my own preconscious and unconscious mechanisms.

So, how would I explain having sensed something? I've recently had the continual sensing of when a particular letter has arrived for me. It is never a matter of wishful thinking as I never sense it arriving on days when it does not, even though I half expected I might. It is not a matter of 'thinking' either because, given logic, in many of these instances, I'd have thought the arrival of one of these letters unlikely and even mentally questioned my sensing. I can only say that I had a sort of body-mapping-based resonance which (on a preconscious level and far more complex than the conscious mind can 'read') had a particular pattern which translated consciously into the sensed knowing that such a letter had arrived.

I remember, too, a time when emotionally I was very comforted by being drawn to the feeling of a person I'd left behind many hundreds of miles away with whom I had no phone contact and knew no mutual friends. I'd had a dream he gave me the colour metallic red. In the post, soon after, a piece of metallic red metal arrived which he'd engraved for me to carry with me and feel I was in his company. Soon after, I'd been watching Katerina Witt win the Olympic ice-dance skating on TV and had gone outside and picked a particular dried purple wildflower which I put in an envelope and sent to this friend. The same week as my flowers were in the post to him, I received a letter from him. He'd been watching this same skater and said it had made him think strongly of me. Enclosed in the envelope were the same purple flowers though not the ones picked by me. Hundreds of miles away, he'd been drawn to pick the same for the purpose before he'd even received mine. We had been resonating with one another.

When people think of psychic ability, they sometimes think of contact with spirits or evil. Being a highly sensing person is about being open to energy either to the sending out of that energy or the receiving of it or both.

The seen and heard and tangible can be sensed as much as the unseen, the unheard and the intangible. Because of this, the (cohesive or dispersed) energy of entities which is no longer contained within the boundaries of a material form are as likely to be sensed as the (cohesive) energy patterns still bound within material forms.

'Evil', too, is just a form of energy, embodied on a material form or not. It is merely an unhealthy, negative, repelling, stagnant and often destructive energy. This type of energy can be sensed by someone whose energy boundaries are open just as 'good' (healthy, positive, attracting, flowing and constructive) energy can be sensed.

In my view, however, sensing beings are less likely to be drawn to 'evil' than those who live primarily within the mind-governed system of interpretation. Whilst certain 'evil' may be soul deep, somehow karmic, most negative energies are the product of spiritual cancer born of false-self neediness within the realm of interpretation.

The greatest fear of evil is that within oneself. Outside of yourself it can't harm you if you aren't drawn to its embrace, through fear or attraction. Even if it is drawn to the light, flowing and positive, the dark, stagnant and negative can't stay if you don't hold it. A one sided embrace on a slippery cliff side won't last long. It is not that evil clings so much as weakness can make the best of people hold it. Just as dust gathers in unswept corners, the negative can't gather in a life full of positivity, flow, change and considered openness.

CHAPTER 16

Why Nobody's Talking

Reading this book you might wonder why people don't talk about these things. There are many reasons, among them fear and folklore but I think there's also a very simple reason why they not only don't but possibly can't.

With the move to consciousness that comes with the acquisition of the system of interpretation, instead of living as a waking subconscious mind, there is a progressive loss of memory of the old system. The mind develops new ways of storing and accessing information and that old system is progressively treated as some redundant, earlier, less developed stage. Yet just because something came from an earlier time doesn't mean it was necessarily useless or even inferior. Simple doesn't have to mean infantile any more than complex necessarily means intelligent. Simple can mean purer, with greater clarity, greater focus, poise and balance.

In a world where the system of sensing has been left behind, few who have moved into the system of interpretation have named the mechanics of the system of sensing. Because of this there is little learned means of putting it easily into words. Even if there were, who'd listen when most people no longer have the mental constructs to slot in such explanation; their minds reformatted, the old disks just can't be read in the new computer.

Another reason why the few who've retained it, don't talk or write about the system of sensing in words people could decipher is fear.

The system of sensing has long been enshrouded in words linking it with images of Ouija boards, crystal balls, palmistry, tarot cards and the mythology of demons, angels and fairy folk. It is portrayed as 'other worldly'. Actually, it is very much an integral and interconnected part of this world in its most holistic sense. Far from being unhealthy, used in a balanced integrated way the system of sensing could be the answer to so much of the spiritual cancer that eats away at the life force of so many people. Rather than being ashamed of 'being like animals', it may be that we'd

125

be better off to be less like screwed up human beings and a little more like well adjusted animals.

Even when there are those who think they've moved beyond these things, the seemingly obscure 'new age speak' of subjects as vast as whales and dolphins, native cultures or crystal healing make some people nervous. Unable to see past the surface of big fish, people with few clothes and not much money, or bits of pretty rock, many people reject exploration of the potential value of some of these things.

Having lost the system, some of these 'new age' interests are the remnants of the system of sensing, still alive in practices on the fringes of society. Without any history in these things, only those with an adventurous streak or those disillusioned with what they have, would give up even an hour of the familiar in favour of exploring the deep.

Fear of the deep is not exclusive to those who've had trouble learning to swim. As a culture which embraces the controllable, the intellectual and the shallow, most will never find the inspiration to explore their own lost civilization.

Getting it Back?

For those interested in rediscovering the system of sensing, where could someone begin?

Many people have begun with things like meditation, yoga, T'ai Chi and certain types of drugs, attempting to tune in by tuning out. Even the relaxation of massage, essential oils, the lighting of candles, can be part of stilling the mind, getting out of a conscious state where mind rules over sensing.

Some people have sought the spiritual through people who claim to 'have the power'. Often believing they, themselves, are not 'special enough', many people let mind undermine their own belief in rediscovering the sensing capacity in themselves. People consult mediums and fortune tellers rather than developing these skills for themselves.

Dreams are a good place to start looking for remnants but first one has to learn to distinguish types of dreams. Many dreams are just mind work – the mind playing out wishes, fears, conflict. This is like the introduction to the story and its middle but it's not its resolution, its conclusion. The subconscious mind can pose questions in words or in pictures just as a conscious mind can. In a waking state, this is called thinking in a conscious state and daydreaming in a preconscious one. A fearful, stubborn or closed mind can dictate the answers, ignoring the greater knowledge and guidance of the soul which has a vaster knowledge of possible answers than the mind can even imagine. A mind which is not dictated by fear is flexible about new directions. Open to knowledge or influence beyond itself such a mind may find itself directed to the answers it may or may not have come up with itself. Even then, the answers may not seem convenient, may not fit into the life one has had passed down, got used to or constructed. Even if the answers are acknowledged in whatever symbolic form they take, it is not so much about letting soul in as it is about having the discipline to let go the control of mind. Even a mind which seeks the right direction may be too arrogant in its assumption that it is superior or that control is necessary, to let go and let soul do the rest. The potential may be there but, contrary to folklore and popular media representation, it may not be that one must put one's mind to developing connection to sensing. Mind has to resign in favour of a shared throne.

Photographic and audiographic memory are about recording information in serial form without filtering it for personal or relative significance. These 'skills' represent a time before mind dictated what was personally relevant and worth taking in and what was not. Photographic memory works like a Camcorder where one can later climb into one's own head and rerun the film like virtual reality. This is like a post-hypnotic state at which time one is seeing with the mind's eye rather than what is around the person at the time of recall.

Audiographic memory is the auditory equivalent, like replaying a tape recording of conversations that took place, songs heard and so on. Scan reading, like photographic memory, is about not filtering information. With suggestion, one can train oneself to 'seek' a particular word on a page and the preconscious mind will eventually be able to scan the page but the focus will fall on the suggested word.

Synesthesia is about sensory crossover where touch or sound can trigger colours or patterns in the mind's eye, where tastes can have shapes or feelings can trigger tastes or smells. Synesthesia comes from a time before fixed sensory integration, before taste was taste and smell was smell, sound was sound, touch was touch and vision was vision. The rigidity of sensory integration is not only a matter of development but also a matter of identity and reinforcement which leads us to insist on using our senses in rigidly defined ways.

Many of us have a whole variety of remnants from the system of sensing but we either fear them, find no place to use them, find no one to share the same experiences with or we're too busy using mind. If you rediscover enough remnants, you can put them together to make a fabric from which you can make something wonderful, possibly even practical.

Problems in the Mechanics

The ideal might be to be equally proficient in the system of sensing as in the system of interpretation and to be able to switch between one and the other as and when needed. But relying on a system of sensing in a world whose structures are almost entirely based on the system of interpretation means that relying on the system of sensing at all would involve problems in the mechanics.

What, for example, would happen to fashion if people found it natural to see beyond the appear to the be it was covering up or hiding?

What of the businesses reliant not just on fashion in all its commercial forms, but on conformist mentality? Those proficient in the system of sensing would sense even the most subtle differences. They'd respond to what was sensed and not unquestioningly, according to conformist stored ideas of good or bad, useful or useless, but to whether a fit was felt between experienced and experiencer, between experienced and a purpose one felt motivated to pursue. Without conformist mentality, economy as it is now known would be threatened with a flexibility it probably could not sustain. So too would other social structures be threatened which were built upon the black and white socially constructed conformist reality of mind. These are the very structures which govern how we relate, prioritize, order and assign. These structures include government, education, law, the media, the family, social class, age, gender, sexuality, culture and race. The politics of interpretation may be a limiter of possibilities, helping stifle creativity but it makes people controllable.

Sensing beyond the appear, and being so proficient in the ability to do so as to take it for granted, would mean being equally unable to shut out this capacity to sense just as most people are now (without drugs or alcohol) unable to shut out interpretation. Would society be plagued with structureless flexible acceptance just as it is now plagued with entrenched, structured prejudice and discrimination? What would happen to the basis of competition in society if the barriers, created by these structures were blown down, redundant? In time, would this structurelessness, flexibility, acceptance, too, become a new form of societal deviance?

Translation Problems

Problems of interpretation between people using one system and those us-ing the other are also likely to occur just as they currently do in bilingual or multicultural environments.

Taking a very simple everyday example. Two people are in a bathroom. As one picks up a fluffy towel after a bath, one may merely have perceived the object in its purely sensory form. At that moment, irrelevant of having interpreted the use of the object, reached for it purely for the sensory expe-rience, wrapping him or herself up in the sensation, becoming part of it, it may not have been interpreted. The other, using interpretation may ask, 'why are you covering yourself up?' Unlike two languages using the same system, sensing and interpretation have no direct translations. How would one set the other straight about these actions without stepping into the world of words, so irrelevant to the system of sensing? Though explana-tion may have no place or relevance in the system of sensing, according to the system of interpretation it would be rude not to answer. The person sensing may see there is a mistranslation and seek to set it right not by ex-plaining but by touching the person with the towel, sharing the sensory experience. The person using the system of interpretation may have no idea why the person has appeared to have been so rude as not to have an-swered, even perhaps assuming this behaviour as some sort of strange, un-expected come-on. Yet by the system of sensing, the person already had answered in the action of sharing the sensory experience of the towel. Even in a society where all were proficient in both systems, society could become polarised, split between those who identified with, valued and more strongly relied on one system or another.

Superiority and Arrogance

Another issue people would have to reflect upon if they rediscovered, and became proficient in, the system of sensing is the current feeling of superi-ority people have over animals, trees and other entities.

Able to merge with these things, they'd experience 'as them', internally rather than externally. The mind-driven construct of superiority would be on shakier foundations. The realisation that humans have become less pro-ficient at this important alternative and less fallible 'intelligence' than the entities humans have always placed themselves above, may give some a bit of an identity crisis. How would we look at our pets, our plants, our ob-jects, even the experience of the 'our' associated with these captured free agents we happened to have convinced ourselves that we possess? How would we reflect on the value of possession when we realise that far from being below this capability, entities proficient in the system of sensing are, with the exception of survival and boundary issues, above it?

'Normality', 'Reality' and 'Humanness'

Our whole idea of perceptual and social reality would become reformed if it was no longer assumed that things are experienced only from without rather than within.

The whole idea of death and life are based on ideas of our separateness to other entities of all kinds, our encapsulation within our bodies. If our boundaries could be shifted, not with mind or body but with will, what would become of all our values and fears regarding life and death? Would we begin to see that some people with live bodies aren't in them and that some begin to go missing from their bodies well before death? What would happen to the values that life is to be cherished and that death is to be feared and the religions which promise salvation from hell. If the experience of God is a sense of absolute equality, belonging and empathic understanding with all things, an experience of joining and a loss of the aloneness of separateness, then what would such religions have to offer to those who could already experience this before death? It is possibly true that as one becomes cut off from the belonging, equality and empathic empathy that comes of the system of sensing, one is perhaps cut off from the experience of what is so enigmatically labelled 'God'. Yet humans continue to pride themselves on their cleverness, on mind. When they speak of animals being without soul, perhaps they, themselves, no longer can tell the difference between mind and soul, or don't dare to, or perhaps to do so has simply become progressively ever more inconvenient.

CHAPTER 17

Imagine

In a world without interpretation, we would be more like animals. However, in a world, devoid of sensing, we are progressively becoming so much less than animals.

With interpretation, animals and plants would perhaps have had the integrity, humility, balance and grace to retain yin's yang, to retain the system of sensing. It is, perhaps, not other entities which need to prove worthy of humans, but humans to prove worthy of the 'God' in all things.

Perhaps this 'God' in all things is that point at which we are not separate, but interconnected, where to disturb the balance of another is to disturb our own on some level, each grain of sand, gradually but progressively creating the sand dune and the sand slide. Humans could be great if they evaluate the word 'great' according to more than a one sided reality of interpretation.

We are invalids and we don't know it. Knowing it is the start of addressing this disability. It takes great strength to admit the master is just the beginner. It takes courageous daring to be vulnerable and open to mergence. It takes enormous skill to be directed by the purity of will devoid of mind and mind's learning. It takes a very big person to be humble enough to let go of the rigidity of defensiveness, hierarchy and superiority. It takes an adventurer to find belonging among that perceived from the outside as 'different'.

Many fear what is different and fear creates rigidity. The avoidance of experience is the avoidance of growth. It is stagnation. It is death within life. To the Xenophobes among and within us all, we'd probably make a good start to accept that there are 'aliens' among us. My advice is, get used to it.